VERSES K

Esa
A tale of strength

Verses Kindler Publication.

VERSES KINDLER PUBLICATION

Verses Kindler Publication.
Website: www.verseskindlerpublication.com

© Copyright, 2024, Ms. Ekta Roopchand

All rights reserved. No part of this book may be reproduced, stored in a retrieval system, or transmitted, in any form by any means, electronic, mechanical, magnetic, Optical, chemical, manual, photocopying, recording or otherwise, without the prior Written consent of its Writer.
Esa - A tale of strength
By: Ms. Ekta Roopchand
ISBN: 978-93-5605-559-9

FICTION STORIES 1st Edition
Price: INR 400/ $20

The opinions/ contents expressed in this book are solely of the author and do not represent the opinions/ standings/ Thoughts of PUBLISHER.

VERSES KINDLER PUBLICATION

DISCLAIMER

This book is written by Ekta Roopchand.

The published work is the original contents of the author and has done her best to edit and make it plagiarism free.

The characters may be fictitious or based on real events but they are not meant to hurt anyone's feeling nor portray anything against any caste or system.

In case of any plagiarized write-up the author is solely responsible for it. The publisher would not be responsible for it.

VERSES KINDLER PUBLICATION

Contents

Prologue 5
Chapter 1: Early days 12
Chapter 2: Navigating Abuse and Gender Inequality 27
Chapter 3: The Trauma of Molestation and Silence 43
Chapter 4: Adolescence and Rebellion 59
Chapter 5: Mentorship and Academic Transformation 80
Chapter 6: Love, Loss, and Resilience 98
Chapter 7: Breaking Away: Career Beginnings and Independence 110
Chapter 8: The Return of Past Demons 122
Chapter 9: Grief, Closure, and Spiritual Awakening 139
Chapter 10: Rebuilding Life: New Beginnings and Future Aspirations 153
Chapter 11: Conclusion 165

VERSES KINDLER PUBLICATION

Prologue

Esa sits, quietly by the window, cradling a cup of tea as the first light starts to break over the horizon. That moment: quiet, one of stillness, in which she wraps herself and listens to the faint sounds of the world waking up as she contemplates her journey. Her eyes trace the pale pink and golden hues stretching across the sky. She smoothes out a wrinkle on her stocking, which feels awkwardly scratched because of a familiar ache that has lived in her heart for as long as she can remember.

The world is yet to wake up, and in this early morning, in the silence, she feels peaceful. Dawn has always been much more for Esa than the dawn of a new day; it symbolizes new beginnings and hope, and the reassurance that no matter how dark the night had been, the light would return.

Sipping her tea, she's lost to years and years, memories defined. She lives one life in Esa, but in reality, she lives several in one: the life she had, the life she fought for, and the life she is building now. But in reflection, she knows there's a common thread that runs through all of it: resilience. It's been her life of survival and transformation, a testament to how much strength found inside herself.

Born into a world of tradition and expectation, Esa's early life was defined by what others wanted her to be. She was schooled in conformity, led down a line long since laid out before she had any say in it. Even as a child, she felt that there must be more than that. A spark, a quiet resistance existed to push her beyond the confines of her upbringing. She felt it as a whisper in her heart, a call to seek out a life that would be authentically a life guided not by rules but by fierce, unyielding spirit.

Esa's mother was the anchor for this wild-eyed girl, the one person who understood her completely. Her mother was soft, a steady presence, and filled with such wisdom, forged through her struggles. She taught Esa to be strong and to believe in herself even when others doubted her. But most importantly, she taught Esa about love—the kind of love that transcends words, that wraps itself around you like a warm blanket on a cold night. When her mother told her that life is a journey and that every twist and turn is an opportunity to learn and grow.

Just as Esa was settling in, she lost her mother. Grief overwhelmed her. It was like a dark, stifling weight crushing upon her soul. She had never felt so alone. She had seen her mother as a guiding light, a confidante, and a haven. It did feel colder, more cruel, in a world with

VERSES KINDLER PUBLICATION

Mom around no more. Those first days after it happened, Esa could not understand why go on. The pain was endless like a storm nobody had warned her was without an end.

But time changed things too. Month after month, something unbelievable went on: Esa started to feel a quiet strength coming from within. It was like her mother's spirit had been seeded inside her heart. She felt she was not alone; that inside her lay the strength to endure. She believed that although the corporeal self of her mother was gone, love, guidance, and teachings had remained within her. Therefore, she would spend the rest of her life living a life of courage, purpose, and love in memory of her mother.

It was at this oppressive time that Esa discovered faith. Reading the Bible was optional at first, almost something that had managed to give her a sense of comfort and meaning amid these dark times. These words spoke to her. Brought comfort she hadn't felt in a long time. She continued reading the stories of perseverance, and hope, of people who had experienced the same horrors and emerged stronger on the other side. She applied these lessons to her life. It was not a blind faith, entangled in dogma and ritual and law. It was an intense personal participation within the larger thing. She took strength in her belief that something greater than simply she existed behind the awful pain she was suffering; that each of her pains and catastrophes was part of some super-wide, divine plan.

Even with all these pursuits of faith, Esa couldn't quite suppress her curiosity about the world around her, either. She saw how faith could bring about division among people. Her belief that was supposed to unite people-turned to be an excuse for lines to be drawn and for differences to separate. She questioned herself many times why, if indeed we all share the same colour of blood, there was such readiness to alienate one another over petty issues of faith. It became a question that stayed in her heart, perhaps one she would never thoroughly understand. She was determined, from the marrow of her bones, to live a life marked not by division but by compassion, by understanding, by an unyielding commitment to love.

She endured her share of rejection as she waded through life. She was turned aside, dismissed, told she wasn't enough, too much, or simply not right. At first, each rejection was like a wound, a reminder of her inadequacies. But with time, she learnt to see rejection very differently. She understood that every "no" was not the end, but a stepping stone to look in and grow further, become stronger. She realized rejection was, in fact, a source of strength. Rejection catalyzes transformation, and though she can't forget the sting of self-doubt that comes with rejection, she wouldn't be able to carry the weight of regret. It was this thought of looking back at her life as a reflection of "what could have been" that filled her with quiet determination to live this life to the fullest. She had come to understand the fact that while rejection could be overcome, regret lingered in the shadow.

This moment was when Esa was at her worst, with the burdens of strife threatening to consume her, and it was at that particular moment when she rediscovered friendship with a lighter light. People like Dora would fill the empty gap left by her mother through her good deeds by bringing meals to Esa, keeping updated on her schedule, checking on her and reminding her of self-care. Dora's presence balm reminded her that even in the middle of loneliness there were people who cared who would step into the darkness with her and offer a hand to hold.

And then there was Maram, who encouraged her to run the first marathon. Together, they crossed that finishing line, and for the first time in a long while, Esa felt she had accomplished something, something like the strength that lay inside of her. Maram was more than a friend; she reminded her of the resilience she had always fought to develop. And in Maram's unshakeable encouragement, Esa saw the resolve of her spirit mirror of her restlessness, reminding herself that she could be stronger than she ever thought possible to be.

Looking back on these friendships, she feels a deep sense of gratitude. For each friend, for every act of kindness, every moment of connection was a reminder that she was not alone. These were individuals to whom she had walked through the darkest of valleys. These were people from whom hope beckoned. They reminded her that love is the greatest power of all, in every shape and form. It was love, after all - love that had carried her through the loss of her mother, love that sustained her through so many rejections and disappointments, and love that gave her enough strength to continue when the road ahead seemed impossibly hard.

Esa sits by the window takes a deep breath and, for the first time, lets her feel the full weight of her journey. She knows that her story is one of resilience, of hope, of finding light in the darkest places. She understands that life, as far as she is concerned, is not about avoiding pain but embracing it: letting it shape you, mould you, and transform you into someone stronger, someone wiser, someone more compassionate. It simply narrates about this journey she learned: that real strength lies not in the absence of vulnerability but in the courage to face it head-on, to let yourself feel, and to rise again.

This book is simply a testament to that journey. It's a story for anyone who has ever felt lost, questioned their worth, and faced rejection and loss. It reminds us all of how great we are, of how we all possess a

VERSES KINDLER PUBLICATION

source of light which takes us through the very darkest of nights. It makes us love the beauty in our flaws, look for meaning in the struggle, and realize that, in the end, love is the most powerful force of all.

As you turn these pages, I hope that you will find a piece of yourself within this story. May it dare you to face your challenges with courage, to seek the beauty in the broken places, and to believe within yourself, for we are all just walking each other home; together we have power enough to light the way.

Chapter 1: Early days

Delhi is the frenetic heartbeat of India; it feels like one giant melting pot on overdrive where ancient and modern cosy up together. It's a cosmopolitan capital with people from every corner of the country and beyond arriving with their stories, languages, and food, oh-the food! Whether you need your fix of chole bhature or sushi, Delhi has you covered. It is a matter of pride for the city that every festival on Earth is celebrated here with a 'more the merrier' attitude.

From fireworks during Diwali to Christmas jingles, Delhi-ites do everything with enough enthusiasm to run the metro on it. What a beautiful balancing act life is here, framed by traditional mores walking shoulder to shoulder with modern lifestyles, with even an elderly aunt trying to figure out Instagram filters. A place where one can see centuries-old monuments standing tall alongside glassy skyscrapers and people running fluent Hindi into street-smart English in a single breath, this cultural cocktail makes Delhi a vibrant, buzzing hub of life where the only thing one cannot find is a dull moment.

This story is of Esa. A girl who was born in Delhi in a multigenerational family to a Catholic mother and a Hindu father.

Her upbringing blended two distinct traditions. The Catholic custom involved weekly visits to church, celebrating Christmas and Easter with prayers, hymns, and festive meals. Baptisms and other Christian sacraments were a part of her mother's spiritual life. On the other hand, her father's Hindu roots introduced her to festivals like Diwali and Holi, temple visits, and rituals involving prayers (pujas), as well as offerings to gods. Hindu customs also included honouring ancestors and participating in family rituals with a strong focus on spirituality and tradition.

Up until the age of seven or eight, she lived in a home where her father and grandfather had a significant influence. Esa's father was a man of discipline and strong principles. He instilled in her the values of tenacity, ethics, and hard work. He gave her little chores to boost her confidence and pushed her to be responsible and independent. Her grandfather was a wise and venerable man who raised her by telling her tales from the past and imparting life lessons about the value of family, humility, and respect for others. This blend of guidance and love shaped her character, creating a strong foundation for her future.

In Delhi, a large number of families reside in cramped neighbourhoods where there is a high need for space. Esa resided in a normal home with eight to ten family members crammed into a small three-bedroom apartment. The constraints of space in such flats often lead to creative and efficient use of every available inch. Each room typically serves multiple purposes: a bedroom may also double as a study or living area, and the kitchen might be compact yet a central hub of daily activity.

In such environments, the dynamics of family life are deeply intertwined. The presence of extended family members, such as an elder brother or grandparents, adds to the communal atmosphere. The layout often involves shared sleeping arrangements and common areas where family interactions are constant. Privacy is minimal, and personal space is limited. Despite these challenges, Delhiites develop a strong sense of community and resourcefulness. The close quarters foster deep familial bonds and a shared sense of responsibility. Cultural practices and traditions, such as joint meals and celebrations, become central to daily life, weaving together the fabric of family and community in these compact living spaces.

They live with her father's elder brother. Esa's uncle was a figure of intimidation in the household. He often resorted to physical abuse to assert control, particularly over the women. His cruelty included frequent verbal insults, harsh physical punishment, and violent outbursts that left lasting emotional scars. He would slam doors, break objects, and use his strength to dominate, creating an atmosphere of fear and tension. His behaviour extended to physical assaults, such as shoving, hitting, and grabbing, leaving women in constant dread and making the home a place of anxiety.

On the other hand, the grandmother was the epitome of kindness and nurturing. Esa handled matters wisely and tenderly, even if the uncle exuded a tinge of malice. Although there was a hint of malice in the uncle's presence, the grandma approached things with tenderness and compassion. She offered comfort with gentle words, soothing embraces, and acts of quiet support. In addition to providing food, her cooking served as a source of emotional warmth and safety for her grandchild, insulating her from the severity of her uncle's actions. The grandmother's ability to establish a haven of love in the middle of the mayhem highlighted the stark contrast between the uncle's cruelty and the kind care she gave, highlighting her function as the family's main source of emotional stability.

Esa was raised in a large, chaotic family and was always shielded from the harsh realities of life by her grandmother, a constant source of love and warmth. Her early upbringing was greatly impacted by the contrast between her uncle's controlling behaviour and her grandmother's nurturing presence.

Her grandmother was a person of steadfast love and generosity. She would get out of bed every morning at four in the morning, establishing a calm yet orderly routine that would set the tone for her day. This early start was a reflection of her strong bond with her granddaughter rather than just a habit. The routine was so integral to their bond that the young girl, despite her tender age, would wake up alongside her grandmother. They would venture out together to fetch milk, a task that symbolised more than just a chore; it was a sacred time of intimacy and shared purpose.

There was one little but cherished ritual that characterized their mornings. Once the milk was collected, the grandma would take her granddaughter to a neighbouring bakery to purchase a cake. This seemingly uncomplicated gesture was actually a deep display of love, providing a brief respite from their home's otherwise constraining surroundings. The cakes served as more than simply a sweet treat; they were the grandmother's way of giving Esa a taste of luxury and affection that she would not otherwise experience. In a family where indulgences like dry fruits and butter were deemed inappropriate for girls, the grandmother defied these norms, ensuring that her granddaughter had moments of sweet delight and nourishment.

This sense of special treatment was not lost on her. She was acutely aware that her experiences were unique from other children's, even at such a young age. She realised that not everyone could share her grandmother's love and the small pleasures she took pleasure in. She felt grateful and privileged as a result of this realization, which increased the value she placed on the time she spent with her grandmother.

When her father got home from work in the evening, he would frequently take her on walks or other outings. Despite his love and attempts to engage her, Esa was adamant about wanting to be close to her grandma. Seeing that she was quite attached to him, her father occasionally enticed her to join him by offering delicacies like ice cream or outings to locations like the deer park. Even though she enjoyed these excursions, she valued her grandmother's security and comfort more. Although her father's actions were sincere attempts to connect with her, they were unable to match the close, unspoken tie she shared with her grandmother.

Esa's rebellious and adamant nature was already apparent at this early age. She had a strong will and was frequently tough to acquire what she wanted because of this, but she also had an outspoken personality. This quality was cultivated by the loving environment her grandmother provided, in sharp contrast to the oppressive one her uncle produced. Her grandmother's affection and care allowed her to express herself and navigate her early years with comfort and confidence.

The contrast between her grandmother's tender care and her uncle's cruelty indicates how difficult her early years were. Her grandmother's protective nature and the small pleasures they shared provided a safe refuge from her uncle's horror and abuse. She had a stronger understanding of compassion and love as a result of these interactions, along with strong emotional resilience that would help her as she grew older. These encounters gave her a deeper appreciation for kindness and love, as well as a solid emotional resilience that would serve her well as she matured.

Till the time Esa was about ten, her perceptions of family relations had been muddled with love and confusion. She addressed her grandmother as "Amma". She called her mother "Aunty" in reflection of her lack of comprehension of titles and relations. This was more than a semantic distinction; it was a symbol of the complex family dynamics with which she contended in her early years.

The cruel ways of her uncle made the home a turbulent and fearful place. His actions were unpredictable and, more often than not, violent, reflecting an underlying anger and a need to control. One of his cruel habits was testing the temperature of tea. Whenever a cup of tea was brought in front of him, he would dip his finger in it to see if it was hot enough, and once it did not happen exactly the way he wanted, he'd sling the full cup on the ground and spread it all over the room. Not only was this an act of discontent with the tea, but also a show-and-tell of his strength and power to show who the boss was and put some fear into those around him. All the mess and destruction were beside the point compared to the humiliation and anxiety he provoked among the people surrounding him.

His violence did not stop there but was also perpetrated in other ways. His wife, in particular, had to suffer at his hands with extreme brutality. The abuse she suffered was both of a physical and psychological nature. There was one incident in particular which left a mark on her that would never fade. One time, he came home late and his wife had already retired to bed. When she got up to attend to his needs, he was angry because it took too long to do this. Merciless in his anger, he punched her several times, with the brutality of the attack causing her nose to swell. Her physical injuries aside, she felt utterly frightened and helpless. She could not eat properly for days because of the ache and swelling of her jaw. Again, that incident brought into the limelight the cruelty involved in the home and the battle for power. This episode also drew a great line of comparison in contrast to the fear and abuse that he would instigate between her father and grandmother-they were her shield of protection, her sanctuary of security and comfort amidst the turmoil. Her father, despite limitations and struggles, would protect her from the worst of her uncle's violence. He played a very complicated role in her life; he was an affectionate father trying to snatch his daughter from hurt amidst an oppressive environment fostered by his brother.

The grandmother's role has been even more pivoting. The bond between the two of them is a great source of strength and stability for her. The instinct of protection and nurturing was behind everything her grandmother did. Her grandmother was that constant source of love and reassurance. She knew how precarious this living situation was and took every precaution to make it a sanctuary for her granddaughter. This was physical protection but also emotional, providing a sense of normalcy and love in a household full of tension and fear.

Every part of their interaction bespoke the grandmother's protective instinct. She made sure that the young girl felt valued and loved to balance out the negativity of the uncle's cruelty. This dynamic, importantly, was allowing the shaping of the girl's early years. In contrast, the brutality of the uncle only underscored and highlighted how solemn and serious the commitment of the grandmother was to the well-being of her granddaughter. Esa's grandmother's love cushioned her from the harsh realities of their home life.

Under such conditions, attempts by the father and grandmother to protect her from her uncle's violence gave her a fragile yet important sense of security. Both struggled to prevent her from seeing or experiencing the uncle's cruel behavior completely. They did so in acts of daily behavior and in sacrifices that were made to ensure her well-being.

Resilience came through in the form of how the young girl resisted such challenges through the love and care provided by her father and grandmother. Together, they created some semblance of normalcy and gave her stability, enabling her to grow up in security despite the turbulent environment. But most of all, she found particular comfort and strength from her grandmother, who showered the girl with affection antipode to the harshness and bedlam of the household.

By the time she was eleven, she had become terribly conscious of how the boys in her home were treated differently from the girls, which truly hurt her and made her angry. Brought up in a traditional ambience, the aura of gender discrimination in bringing up the children was loud and clear, which was quite disconcerting to her.

In Esa's home, the way men and women were brought up varied in large ways and manners. Boys, who included cousins and uncles, enjoyed privileges and freedom not accorded to girls. An example includes new clothes and other personal indulgences that are more often than not reserved for the male component of the family. This is not just a question of material possessions but, from a broader perspective, a cultural bias that places higher value on male members.

The difference was stark in regards to new clothes. The boys would get new clothes very frequently, while girls were given worn-out clothes or low-quality clothes. New clothes for boys, especially during festivals or special occasions, were usually of high quality and more fashionable, which indicates that they were valuable to the family. Girls were given hand-me-downs or given lower-quality attire. The expectation was that girls must be content with what they had been given and not desire more. This was not superficial but reflected a deeper problem of gender-based partiality.

The injustice didn't stop at the material goods; the expectations regarding society and family were also worlds apart. While boys could go to schools or colleges, it was presumed that their futures were so important they deserved investment; they could find their interests and skills without big restrictions. Girls were commonly confined to domestic roles and expected to pay more attention to household chores than to their personal objectives. Social norms regarded being a caretaker and a homemaker as their main role, thus limiting girls' potential.

This inequality was further emphasized in daily interactions and expectations in the household: whereas boys could often be viewed with a lighter eye, thereby being watched with respect, girls had to play strictly according to the rules and display more obedience. While boys easily escaped reprimand or even forgiveness for their mistakes, girls' mistakes were seriously taken to task. This further led to situations where boys felt entitled to privileges while girls felt pressured into following restrictive norms.

This was not just a question of privilege and expectation in the difference in treatment, but also how emotions and behavior were managed. Boys were encouraged to be assertive and independent, and girls were expected to be demure and compliant. Such gendered behaviour furthered the notion that boys' needs and desires were more valid and worthy of attention than those of girls.

Esa was increasingly irritated by the inequalities that she had to encounter. It is this difference in doling out less-than-new clothes and other privileges that made her feel less valuable and not treated fairly. She did not like being at a point where she could see and understand that gender norms permeated into every level of life and constricted her options. Such unfair treatment did little but build more resentment in her and a yearning for change and equality.

In other words, at the tender age of eleven, she had painfully realised the gender-based inequities marking her upbringing. Even the very difference in treating boys and girls material possessions like new clothes to larger expectations placed upon girls by society-was indicative of a systemic bias tending to marginalize female members of the household. This realisation is a cause of much distress for her as she grapples with limitations imposed by conventional gender roles and the unfairness of her situation. Her increased awareness of these inequities launched a more profound understanding of greater societal issues affecting her and fueled her desire for a more equitable and just environment.

She realized through small moments on many occasions when she was young that her family was poor. She remembered how her mother was budgeting every single rupee and just how frequent conversations about saving money on just about anything were. The simple meals and fights over bills not paid spoke volumes about their monetary situation.

Esa's father was a cycle repairman, an occupation that lay central to putting bread in their mouths. He was uneducated but very astute; he often worked from morning to night, repairing bicycles continuously for sufficient money to make a decent life for his family. There was something basically entrepreneurial about him in the way he could lure customers and manage a small business with no formal education.

These laid the skeleton of her early understanding of work and ambition. The father's tireless work ethic and resourcefulness taught her the use of perseverance and the drive for success that he could flourish with so little helped instil in her a respect for hard work and a drive to overcome obstacles, thus nurturing her view of ambition and making a better life.

She struggled with a knot in her stomach inside the family home. It was only in her grandmother's arms that she felt safe for the first time. The grandmother became this nurturing, warm presence that enveloped her and kept the fright, danger, and chaos away. These minor acts, done tenderly between the two, like fetching milk every morning, created security and normalcy in an unstable world.

This feeling of safety was always tinged, however, with an undercurrent of confusion and fear. Tension was always so palpable in this household, acting like some sort of constant reminder of the volatile atmosphere her uncle's harsh behavior had cultivated. The noise of arguments, the fear of his unpredictable rage, and the visible distress from her mother created an atmosphere of unease. As comforting as her grandmother made her feel, she couldn't leave herself blind to the underlying tension at the core.

She felt grateful for the protection she received, yet at the same time was anxious about those uncertain threats looming over her. It is this duality that has kept Esa trapped between the comforting embrace of her grandmother and the perpetual fear instilled by the harsh dynamics of their household, leading to deep-seated confusion on the plane of safety and stability.

Chapter 2: Navigating Abuse and Gender Inequality

Esa's world began to crack open when she was just 11 years old. The life revealed some bitter truths which she always knew but never fully comprehended. She wasn't a child anymore. Blissfully, she was unaware of the unfairness around her. But now she could see the deep lines dividing men and women in her family.

One of the sharpest memories crystallizing this understanding for her was related to the day when new clothes were given out in the household. Every time new clothes came into the house, they were given to Esa's cousins and brothers, who were about her age. These new sets of clothes were crisp, bright, and clearly chosen with care. Her cousin's brothers pranced around in them proudly, and everyone praised them. They said how good they looked and how they were growing into fine young men. But Esa got a hand-me-down outfit that was ill-fitting, dingy, and obviously passed down. The message would not be missed: boys were to be fatted up and given the best there was from the family, but girls would have to make do with leftovers.

At the time, Esa said nothing.

She stood there, silent, holding the old dress, her small hands shaking with the frustration that would not find an outlet. She looked up at her grandmother for some form of recognition, perhaps a little solace, and her grandmother merely patted her hand as if to say, "This is how it is." That wordless passing of looks became one of the themes in her life. It was as if her grandmother understood her frustration but was too bound by tradition to challenge it.

Another frightening incident that passed through Esa's life is when she was sitting under her bed sheet, reading a Champak comic by the light of a torch. Her grandmother was sleeping in the room; her father had gone to do business somewhere. Esa adored the hours that went that way; she plunged herself into the story, though she knew she wasn't supposed to read comics-these 'boy' comics, in particular.

The still night was roughly torn apart by the thudding of heavy footsteps. Her uncle had just come home from an argument with his wife, drunk as a horse. He caught a glimpse of Esa curled up in her bed with the comic spread open on her lap. The frown deepened. He walked toward her with squinting eyes, drunkenly disapproving.

Without a word, he turned away and walked toward the gate of the house. Esa stared, perplexed but still hoping he would leave her alone. She could see him there through the door, lighting a cigarette and puffed with furious intentions into the cold night air. Maybe it was because he saw her reading.

Only moments passed before he again bust in the house, his eyes wild and furious. Esa didn't react in time. He grabbed her by the arm and yanked her from bed, dragging her toward the gate. "Stand still," he hissed, his breath heavy with the sharp, bitter scent of alcohol.

Scared stiff, Esa froze, her body shaking as her uncle took another drag from his cigarette. Without any warning, he pressed the lit end of it against her right wrist. The searing pain was unlike she had ever felt before. Esa screamed, tears streaming down her face.

"Quiet!" he growled, "if you scream again, I'll do it again."

Esa's heart was thrashing, the ache in her wrist as the cigarette rose from his lips. She could smell the beer on his breath-a choking reek of smoke and booze that filled her lungs and wanted her to flee, escape, but she couldn't. She tried to squirm away from him; her uncle was too strong. He thrust her back, so her arm lay along her side. He leaned forward, letting the smoke from the tip caress her, then lift it to draw back so he could do it again.

By this time, Esa's screaming had become so loud that her grandmother woke up. She rushed out of the house to find her granddaughter crying in the dark. The night air was icy, but Esa's skin burned. No one said a word; her grandmother just embraced her with an embracing hug and pulled her away from the guy who had terrorized her.

There were three red angry burn marks on Esa's right wrist. The moonlight would not tell her why he did this. She was lost in what made him do it. When had he felt this rage? The episode was totally meaningless, cruel, and unforgettable.

From that point on, Esa's grandmother locked the bedroom door at night, in case she didn't get back before sleep started calling. Maybe their bedroom might keep these terrors out of them, she thought, but deep inside Esa knew that the abuse wasn't going anywhere. It would only be a matter of when.

Those will be the marks she will take through the rest of her life-three burn marks that remind her of this night when those who were meant to protect her were now absent.

The issue of food was another constant reminder of how different life was for boys and girls in her family. hen anything special came to eat-dry fruits, sweets, or butter, boys in the house got it first. They would be set before a plate piled high, while the girls received modest portions or sometimes nothing at all. It was always explained as "boys need more to grow" or "girls don't need so much." Esa watched as her male cousins gorged on the best food while she and the other girls many times went without. It wasn't the hunger that disturbed her; it was the sheer this feeling of being inferior only because she was a girl. One night, her grandmother surreptitiously slipped her a piece of bread with butter when no one else was paying attention. Esa looked up at her grandmother in great appreciation, but upon taking a bite of the bread, it tasted bitter-the bitterness of all that was going on. Did her grandmother have to hide her small acts of goodness? Why was she not entitled to the same perquisites as her male cousins?

She was still trying to understand how it was so unfair that the boys in her family always got new clothes, while she and all the other girls got only leftovers when something happened that shook her to the core.

If Esa would serve tea to her uncle, her hands would shake a little. The way her uncle would take the cup and dip his finger into it just to see if it was warm or not. One evening, when she did this again, her uncle dipped his finger and frowned forthwith. Displeasure darkened his face as he found the tea cold. Without a word, he flung the cup on the floor, the hot tea splashing in all directions. "Make it again," he growled. Had it been his wife, he would have thrashed her. She saw the way her uncle treated the women in the house. A scowl on his face would send a wave of fear around the room. Esa looked up at her aunt with tears trapped in her eyes. Her aunt did not protest but stooped to clean up the mess and went to make another cup of tea. Esa's heart was racing in anger, yet she did nothing but keep quiet-helpless in the real world controlled by men like him. She wanted to scream-to tell him it wasn't fair. But her grandmother, standing beside her, laid a soothing hand on her shoulder, holding her back. "He'll only get angrier," her grandmother whispered, resignation heavy in her voice.

But the tea was the least of the violence.

Esa's uncle had a short fuse, and it was usually shortest late into the night when he came home drunk.

Esa's aunt had learned to bear his abuses silently, but many times, the violence had escalated to unbearable levels.

Then, one night, he came home much later than usual.

Esa's aunt, knackered after a day of endless chores, had already retired to bed. When she didn't open the door fast enough, he kicked it open himself and stormed into the bedroom. What followed was a terrifying barrage of punches and kicks. Esa lay awake in the next room and heard the muffled thuds, her aunt's sobs. She wanted to run to her, to protect her, but she was just a child. All she could do was curl up under the covers and pray it would stop. The next morning, the aunt was able to barely eat with a swollen nose. In that fashion, as if their silence could make it not have happened in the first place, no one spoke about it. But for Esa, her aunt's bruised face was an instant reminder that the violence had just simmered beneath their household boil. As Esa grew older, her understanding of gender inequality deepened through more painful experiences, particularly in the form of abuses levied at the women in her family. The uncle was a tyrant who ruled the household with an iron fist, especially over his wife and the other women. Perhaps one of the most seared memories in her mind was the way he would treat his wife, Esa's aunt, over matters as minute as hell. In all that, Esa found solace in her grandmother. She was the only one who made her feel safe when the world appeared to fall apart.

Whenever her uncle's temper flared, her grandmother quietly led Esa away, taking her either to the kitchen or into the garden, shielding her from the worst of the violence.

There were nights when Esa woke up to the shouting of her uncle, only to feel her grandmother's soft hand on her back, drawing her closer and saying, "It is okay.

The warmth and comfort came from her grandmother, who tried to stand between Esa and the ugliness in the household. She would hold her close to her body and shield her from the worst of it, making sure that Esa was never the target of her uncle's rage directly. But even at 11, Esa had an inkling that her grandmother's protection only stretched that far. The silent rules of their house dictated that men's anger and authority were what prevailed, no matter the level of resistance posed by the women. Yet, even the protection given by her grandmother had its limits. While she was doing her best to shield Esa from possible harm, there were instances when Esa could not help but suffocate under the weight of a male-dominated household.

Her grandmother was, after all, just another woman bound by the same rules and limitations that governed Esa's life.

All attempts of protection by the older woman only contributed to Esa's growing belief that women are to endure, be silent, and know their place.

Yet, as young as she was, Esa's heart was already filled with quiet defiance. She was not just to sit back and accept such a life of inequality. And it was then, while watching her aunt patiently bear her uncle's cruel nature, that stirred something deep inside her- a fire growing to get even stronger when she started questioning everything. Even at 11, Esa knew she did not want to be like the other women who came before her. The more aware Esa became of the inequality that surrounded her, the more frustrated she became. She was no longer satisfied standing in the background and watching her aunt berated, her male cousins treated her more favourably, and her female family members always put down. She began pushing back in small ways. It was that afternoon when he had flung another cup of tea on the floor, shouting at his aunt to remake it, that Esa could no longer hold it in. She stepped forward, her slight frame trembling with the fury. Why do you treat her like that?" she insisted, her voice trembling but loud enough to take note. Her uncle turned to her, eyes narrowing in a wide-eyed surprise. Nobody ever talked back to him, let alone a girl.

"Go to your room," he growled.

But Esa didn't budge. "It's not right," she said this time, her voice clearer and firmer. "She is not your servant.

The room fell silent for a moment. Esa's aunt stared at her with incredulous eyes; her uncle, with shock at the audacity of her words, began to take a step toward her, his dark face darkening further in anger. Esa's heart thundered, but she refused to be cowed.

The moment her grandmother appeared, she pulled Esa back and whispered fiercely in her ear, "You'll only make it worse. Go."

Reluctantly, Esa retreated, but not before the damage was fully done. Her uncle had never forgotten, and since then, he kept a closer eye on her, his patience for her outbursts growing thinner with each passing day.

As years went by, Esa continued to develop her understanding of gender roles: the silenced, obedient, self-sacrificing women versus the men who were allowed to dominate and control. It was deeply inculcated into the fabric of their lives, but Esa refused to accept that.

Her childhood experiences of favouritism, abuse, and unequal treatment fueled an ever-pressing urge inside of her to counteract expectations placed on a girl. She didn't know quite how, but she knew she was going to somehow break loose from the vicious cycle that thus far dictated the pattern of her life.

She had to witness emotional and physical abuse, leaving deep scars yet instilling a fierce sense of determination.

She saw as clear as daylight the atrocity that was occurring; it set a fire in her that, as she grew older, would only be burningly stronger.

She would no longer remain silent.

She would no longer accept this as "how things are." And even though being protected by her grandmother had been a comforting thing, Esa intuitively knew real change would never come about through protection but rather through full-on confrontation.

These early experiences of gender discrimination and abuse shaped Esa's understanding of the world in profound ways. The reality was less than that, and violence was one surefire way of making sure they stayed there, instilled into her from an early age. These things opened her fire rather than breaking her. She was determined to change the already entrusted roles assigned to her and turn down the silence brought upon her.

Where the path ahead was misty, one thing was certain: she would not be hobbling with the same chains that had enslaved the women in her family for generations. She would fight, and not just for Esa's world, which was a silent battle, with anger and frustration bubbling underneath the surface, yet she felt powerless to express any of those emotions. It gnawed at her daily that in her family, boys were given better treatment than the girls. It wasn't anymore about clothes or food; it was something deep inside of her. With every little injustice, heavier and heavier, her chest felt as if invisible chains bound her to a world that neither had fitted nor agreed upon.

She had long watched as boys were celebrated for the smallest of achievements, given new clothes, extra servings at the table, and praised for simply existing. As for her and the other girls, they were to quietly accept their place and be grateful for whatever little they were given. They were never praised, only instructed. The inequality was choking, and at just 11 years of age, Esa's mind was abuzz with thoughts and questions to which she didn't have an answer.

Years later, her internal fight made the struggle more evident: on the one hand, Esa certainly felt a boiling, seething anger in her guts toward the world that enveloped her. The injustice was too loud to tune out. She began to see the silent rules that controlled her family, where men deserved more and women less, and women had to earn even the right to ask.

Her mind screamed in protest such silent oppression, yet she felt trapped. No matter how stormy anger brewed inside her, the realists of her situation left her helpless; her uncle's temper was like a storm that would always sweep through the household unpredictably. She had become so accustomed to seeing her aunt walk on eggshells around him, trying in her own way, most impoverished, to steer clear of his anger. But no matter how hard she tried, somehow, it was just never good enough. The incident of the tea cup thrown to the floor and her uncle striking his wife-had left an indelible mark upon Esa's young heart.

She had seen it all, small and helpless, frozen while her aunt received punishment for some minor error. That night in bed, the weight finally fell on Esa. Anger burned in her chest, though fear and powerlessness kept her silent. She despised the way her uncle treated the women of the family and resented how powerlessly they all seemed to stand in his presence. But what could she do?

She was just a girl in a world where girls did not count for much. She had seen her aunt, her mother, and even her grandmother, who was as strong as she had been, succumb to such unfair treatment. They had learned to survive in this world, but Esa didn't want to simply survive; she wanted more and wanting more felt like a dangerous thought. Esa's grandmother was the only source of warmth in her life; she seemed to understand the unfairness of their situation without saying a word. She would pull her aside whenever she could, giving her more food when no one was looking or protecting her from her uncle's wrath. It was these small gestures of affection that made Esa feel safe, but even her grandmother's protection had limits. But however hard her grandmother tried; the way things were could not be changed.

VERSES KINDLER PUBLICATION

Men ran things, and women sidestepped. Women bent, never broke. But Esa did not want to bend. Growing up and accepting this life was a thought filling her with dread. She watched her aunt, her mother, and even the other women of the family- the life she knew she did not want. Still, she could not accept that her life was only one consequence of the whims of the men surrounding her.

But how was she to change things when everything around her told her to keep quiet and to know her place? This only irritated her as the years went by. The more she saw, the more Esa realised that her anger was not her own but an anger carried by generations of women beforehand- an anger that had been silenced. And even in her most powerless moments, it stirred within her a determination unshakeable: a determination quietly to change her fate. She didn't know how but knew she couldn't live in this environment forever. Esa understood that her anger was more than just a feeling; it was the fuel. It forced her to pay attention, observe, and question everything. Why must the boys be given more? Why must the women be punished simply for living? In her head, she ran these thoughts as she watched her family, her mind gradually coming awake to the fact that things didn't have to be this way. She started to dream of a life in which she could make her own decisions, in which her value was not tabulated by her gender. For now, these dreams were far-off, hazy images that consoled her during the blackest moments.

As of now, she could not change her reality yet, but the seed had been sown.

Esa was not just angry; she was determined.

Although she had not known it at the time, it was that resolve that would be the key to unlocking another future, one in which she would have her freedom from the shackles of inequality tightly binding women for so long in her family.

VERSES KINDLER PUBLICATION

Chapter 3: The Trauma of Molestation and Silence

Esa's world was full of silent battles in which anger and frustration had been simmering beneath the surfaces, yet she felt she could not let them out. She always felt that something was wrong in her house. But she could not pinpoint what it was. There was an ongoing reminder that the boys in her family were treated better than the girls. And that nagged at her daily. It was no longer just about clothes and food anymore. They were given freedom, which only she and her sister could imagine. It was not just that; it was something much deeper. She could feel that there was inequality within her family. She had long listened while boys were rewarded for the smallest achievement, simply for breathing. She and the rest of the girls received no such fête; they were expected to remain content with their station, grateful for whatever they got. The girls were never to be congratulated but only to be instructed.

She often wondered why the boys should be treated as princes and she and her sister as though they did not exist.

Esa's mind was filled with questions. Unfortunately, she never gets them answered. But this thing she cannot ignore. Inequality was everywhere. It clung to the walls of her house like a stubborn stain. This was shaping the lives of everyone who lived there. Every small injustice chime in with a weighty insinuation onto her chest. It was like invisible chains binding her to a world she did not feel belonged to or even agreed with. But it was not just material things. It was the way her uncle, a shadow lurking in every room, treated the women of the family.

Her uncle was a tyrant, and the women had to serve him. The temperature of the tea mattered more to him than his wife's broken nose. His was a selfish world governed by his own personal needs. He cared hardly for anyone, not the ladies of the house. Cruelty and callousness were his worst traits; nothing mattered but himself. What matters most is that nothing about others did, especially the women. Her uncle's anger would blow from nowhere like a storm all over the house.

Esa had grown used to her aunt tiptoeing around him, doing her best not to provoke his ire. But the more desperately her aunt went about trying to avoid provoking his wrath, the more it seemed the less good it was. Many of such incidents had left deep scarring on Esa's young heart. She saw the scene playing out, feeling incapable and powerless, standing petrified as her aunt was punished for a small blunder. The fear was constant, but they never talked about it-they just endured.

There was an increasing tension within her as she progressed through age.

As she seemed to be getting older, her internal battle was showing more on the outside.

In one sense, she felt a deep anger toward everything around her. The injustice of the whole situation was too loud to ignore. She had started to see the unwritten rules governing her family as well-intentioned, they said that men deserved more, and women had to deserve it to even ask. Esa's mind screamed against the quiet oppression, but she was powerless. No amount of poison could be brewed in her mind enough to counter the reality of the situation for her. That night, when Esa went to bed, the weight of it all was crushing.

Anger rose up inside her, filling her chest, but fear and hopelessness kept her tongue still. She hated how her uncle treated the women of the family, and how he took their power from them. But what could she do? She was only a girl, anyway-a girl in a world where girls did not count as much. She had seen her aunt, mother, and even grandmother, who was as robust as one could imagine, submit to such an unfair treatment. One had to learn how to survive in this world, but Esa wanted more than survival; it felt like a dangerous thought, wanting more. The only source of warmth for Esa was her grandmother, the only person who would seem to understand that things weren't being fair without really having to say it. Her grandmother pulled her aside sometimes and stopped her. She was the shield for Esa, which made her very safe, but the protection by her grandmother was not limitless. No matter how much a grandmother fought or tried, nothing changed the way things had to be. It was in the hands of men, and around it, the ladies had to go bowing but not breaking. Esa did not want to bend though.

She would think of growing up living this sort of life; she'd be scared to death, and she could see her aunt, her mom, and even other females in the family who knew that wasn't the kind of life she wanted. She did not accept that her whole future was destined to be dictated by the whims of the men around her. But how could she when all around her told her to hold her tongue, to accept her place? The more she saw, the more Esa realised that her anger was not hers alone; it was the anger of many women before her, an anger that had been silenced for generations. Though sometimes powerless, deep inside her, something began stirring, a quiet but unshakeable determination to change her fate. How she did not know, but surely, she couldn't live in this environment anymore.

Esa began to realize that her anger was far from just a feeling—it was fuel. It sparked inside her to be paying attention, observing, and questioning everything. Why should the boys be favoured? Why should the women be punished for just being there? These thoughts swirled in her head while she watched her family, her mind slowly waking up to the thought that maybe things don't have to be like this.

She started dreaming of a life in which she could make her own choices, and her worth was not dictated by gender.

But for now, the dreams were hazy pictures she used to take comfort in the darkest hours. She could not yet change her reality, but the seed had been planted. Esa was mad; above all, she was determined. And though she did not know it at the time, that resolve would unlock a different future, one in which she could break the shackles of inequality that had long ensnared the women in her family. It was normal that there was fear in Esa's house, but something much darker, lurked beneath the surface. It took her years to piece together the full horror of what had been happening.

It began with the bathroom, one of only a few rooms in the house, and not one given to individual use.

It was one day when Esa's aunt noticed that something didn't seem right. Every time one of the girls went to take a bath, her uncle was nowhere to be found, but she would find him within a few minutes just near the bathroom door. She started to be suspicious, and so she decided to follow him. What she found left her in shock. There was a small hole inside the bathroom through which her uncle had been spying on the girls as they bathed. He had been working for years in this manner. This realisation, like a punch to the gut, hit Esa's aunt, but she did not confront him. Instead, she quietly mended the hole in the wall. She said nothing to anyone except Esa's mother, whispering the secrets of that night in the dead of night. The family could not afford to stir the waters. That uncle would bring shame, and in their community, family honour came before the safety of its women.

But that was only the starting point.

Esa opened her eyes one night to something tugging at her dress.

She was drowsy, half-asleep, but there he stood-at the foot of her bed-his hand grasping at the fabric of her dress. Before she could make a sound, he turned out of the room, leaving her shivering in the darkness. She couldn't find the words to say it when morning came.

Who would believe her? Even if they did, what could they do? The women in her family were powerless, and Esa felt powerlessness seeps into her bones. The abuses did not end there. Her uncle's hands always somehow found a way to reach her when they were alone, and each time they did, Esa felt increasingly caged in. Her aunt knew something was wrong. She warned Esa, telling her to be careful and avoid being alone with him, but what could she do? It wasn't like she could leave the house. Where would she go?

His disgusting behaviour was not only to the women in the house but also to the housemaids. He treated them with the same disrespect he had toward the women in his family.

He would stare at them at work; sometimes, under false pretences, he would get close to them. Many times, he would attempt to grope them or make bad comments to them and leave them humiliated and helpless. The maids, reliant on their income, could only share fearful glances with each other and remain silent. They knew complaining would amount to little in a home where his mistreatment was ignored, leaving them powerless to prevent his unwanted favours each day.

VERSES KINDLER PUBLICATION

Esa's father was a good man, at least according to what everyone says about him. He worked hard, building the company from the ground up, and making ends meet for his family. But he was dumb to what was happening in his own house. He trusted his brother too much, thinking him to be the pillar of strength in the family. Esa's father did not know that he had misplaced his trust in the man whom he believed was the same who tortured his daughters.

Her mother was fighting a different type of battle. Besides, she was a Catholic in a family Hindu. That alone put her at odds with everyone around her. The family of the uncle, where their children were taken to live, hated her, calling her the worst insults behind their backs- witch prostitute, the outcast. However, Esa's mom would not have it. She strongly believed in what she was and refused to let the constant insults break her spirit. Still, sometimes Esa could see how everything weighed her mother down. She was so afraid of it.

Years go by, and with it grows Esa, but the wound of childhood does not disappear.

The family of Esa's father possessed a strong feeling of malice toward her mother, often telling her some filthy abominable comments about her.

They called her a witch, and a prostitute-these were crimes filled with prejudice and hatred. These abusive words were not whispered behind closed doors; rather, they were explicitly communicated and made the surroundings hostile for Esa and her family. Such derogatory comments reflected their detestation of her mother's faith as well as her unwillingness to give in to their expectations. The continuous wave of abuses hurt Esa immensely, widening her feelings of alienation as well as emphasizing the deep gap between her parents' two families. This was when her brother entered her life; he was 4 or 5 years younger than her.

At 17 or 18, her parents moved into their own house, but her father was persistent in trying to connect her with his family and his culture and kept telling her how important tradition was. However, what remained unseen to her was a silent battle between her parents, who belonged to different faiths. The father, perhaps with an optimism to believe otherwise, was keen to merge two worlds, but the mother did not budge on her faith or her happiness. It was a common affair which would create discomfort in the household. The years ticked by and passed away without ever addressing the differences that appeared between them, yet somehow did slip away.

Another decade passed, but Esa's bond with her siblings deepened and grew more meaning-rich. She was very close to her younger brother who connected to her differently from her sister. Her sister, on the other hand, gradually became more inclined towards her mother's culture and belief and closed closer to the mother's worldview. This growing closeness led to silent distance despite their shared upbringing and the home that they both shared. Instead, Esa became closer to her brother. Maybe because, between them, there were both of them who had to contend with the issues or tensions between the two faiths and expectations from their parents' end. Although the family was not often relaxed because of the tension that was looming at times, it was in the company of her brother that Esa became close to sharing a sense of warmth within the household full of emotional complaints.

When Esa's mother decided to leave, she did not say much about it to anyone.

She had just very silently taken Esa's little sister and was leaving, taking nothing with her except that Esa had to care for her little brother. The house kept on falling into an eerie quietness days before their departure, as if each one had known that something was about to be changed, but no one dared to say about it. Her mother, unmoved, stood by the door and turned to Esa to say one last thing: "You are smart, Esa. You will figure this out. Take care of yourself." It was neither encouragement to stay nor words of truce but the hard truth delivered candidly. There, holding his hand, Esa was stunned, torn inside.

She was entrusted not only with caring for him but also with the all-consuming feeling of abandonment. Words from her mother stayed in her head as she wandered. Empowering yet lonely. Although the responsibility she felt bore the weight of her mother's trust in her intelligence, it also brought him a painful realization: she was now alone. Esa closed the door behind her mother and sister, knowing he had little choice but to step up to the challenge. She had to find her way to care for her brother and for herself in this new world, which suddenly felt so much larger and lonelier. Esa's sister was two years younger than her, and she stayed with their mother after separation.

Not only had their marriage been split; but the family system also was split apart during the separation between Esa's parents. Their father, whose anxiety and irritation were sharply raised by the constant negative commentary and judgment from family members about his estranged wife, would always worry about the impact this might have on the younger daughter. He feared that the discriminatory comments and prejudices might influence her perception of her mother and the strained relations with her family. This concern added to his already heavy emotional load because he was faced with the prospect of raising Esa and her brother in an atmosphere infected by conflict and contempt. The father's concern about his younger daughter underscored deep fractures in the family and hindered any sense of normalcy after a long period of discord. And so Esa did what she had been doing since she was ten years old: she survived. She took care of her brother, kept him away from that poisonous family she'd escaped, and did her best to cobble together a life for herself. But the damage was done and a lifetime of tragedy clung to her like a shadow, never leaving her completely.

One day, sitting with her inwardly reflecting on the passing years, Esa realized an important thing. That long heat burning inside of her was not just anger: it was fuel. What had kept her going drove her to pursue a better life - where she wouldn't be silent any more.

Esa knew she had to break that cycle.

The world she grew up in was one that silenced women, whose silence allowed men like her uncle to thrive, so she had to become the voice that her younger self had needed all those years ago. She would have fought back, not by violence, but by her voice, her strength, and by her determination to carve out a future that wasn't defined by her past. As Esa thought back to her childhood, she realized that all the abuse and the pain had tried to shape her, breaking her apart. Still, it had not broken her. She survived, found a stronger voice out of survival, where she stood up for herself for her own, not just herself, but every girl silenced, every woman who was ever told to quiet down, and to endure it all.

Esa's stormy life has impacted, in a gigantic way, her thinking about trust and people in authority in her family and neighbourhood. The home had not been without abuse, hypocrisy, and everyday confrontations. Consequently, she made a deep, unashamed scepticism toward people who assumed power and influence.

Esa witnessed extreme differences based on gender from a young age.

The depth at which her uncle's abuse had become the order of his day and how he could insult all women, from his housemaids to her aunt, brought an end to any romantic notion she ever held that anyone holding a position of power was somehow good or just by default. Seeing firsthand the tantrum of her uncle, spilling his tea on the floor due to his anger, then turning to inflict upon his wife the exact same kind of abuse or worse, really exposed Esa to how little she knew. It was ironically these people who were supposed to offer protection and dole out justice, but who instead became sources of pain. This disillusionment extended into her family dynamics as well. Her father's family constantly vilified her mother with vile accusations and undermined her respect for her paternal relatives. Their severe judgments and cruel words portrayed what authority and familial loyalty were built to be: it was a place of conditional love and respect, where their biases and prejudices would override all else.

This only made Esa much more distrustful as she grew up, further alloyed with feelings of betrayal by her mother's departure from her life and her inability to protect her from the hostility of the family.

Her mother's sudden disappearance with her younger sister, leaving Esa behind and even adding to the feelings of abandonment, plunged her into the harsh reality of her family's ruined state. The promises her mother made became a shibboleth of empowerment, a vow that also jabbed at loneliness: "You're smart, Esa. You'll figure it out. Take care of yourself." Those words always echoed. Whereas relating to authority is the other side of her personality, Esa displayed skepticism as she interacted with leaders, community figures, or mentors. Betrayal and exploitation cut across much of her early life and affected the trust she could have directed toward any mentor, leader, or community figure. This resulted in conflict in her, as she once needed help but would fear being disappointed or abused. Instead, this skepticism dogged her approach to people's integrity and intentions, thereby making it difficult for her to form trusting relationships.

Furthermore, the large religious war between her parents and the social pressure heightened her sense of mistrust. The incessant negative comments about her mother and the war inside were making her feel that authority was neither correct nor just. Her father's fight to cling on while her family condemned him to hell was somewhat similar to her inner struggle with accepting any authority or guidance.

It was Esa's experiences that shaped her into one who approached trust with such disdain. She learned, instead of placing faith in external figures, to increasingly rely on herself and her judgment and instincts. This self-reliance became a means of dealing with life, which often presented her with hypocritical authorities or authorities possessed of malice.

In the end, Esa's lifetime of being belittled at an early age made her distrustful of authority figures-whether that was the family members or the community itself.

The humiliation she endured and witnessed made her not just of integrity but also of the intentions of those who were in power. Through these tests, she was able to learn ways and means of finding a balance between her longing to connect with an approach that is a bit guarded toward trust. In turn, she became a resilient person who had learned the hard way that true authority and support must be earned through real respect and understanding.

So, in the end, Esa knew that her story was never about survival alone; it was about resilience and strength in the darkest of places and a refusal to define itself through wounds that dare not speak their names. She was more than the girl who had been hurt; she was the woman who had learned to heal, and that, in turn, was the most powerful thing of all.

Chapter 4: Adolescence and Rebellion

There was an evening when Esa observed schoolchildren who were returning home, and their laughter was reflected through the streets. The memory of school life began to fill her mind. For most people, school is a place where children find their first friends, their dreams, and a building ground for the future. But for Esa, school was just the opposite. It was never a place filled with joy, laughter, or excitement. But she was not at home: she felt like an outsider in this setting, totally dislocated from all those who surrounded her. She was a backbencher, not out of an intention to avoid attention but out of a long-standing realisation of the fact that she did not belong.

Esa learned about loneliness from life at home. Her father was always working. She was left all alone to spend her days in isolation. Her younger brother was around; he was far too small to grasp what his sister had to undergo. School should have been a respite for her, but it seemed like jail. Jail walls made of indifference, the deafening silence between her and all her classmates.

Every morning, she dragged herself to school because she was interested in learning but because there was no other choice. She was invisible, slipping through the cracks of the school system. The teachers barely noticed her, and the other students seemed to live in a world that she couldn't access. As they forged friendships, laughed in the corridors, and shared their lives with one another, Esa found herself invisible. She was never too great at studies and was not motivated to perform well. Lectures were long, never-ending lines that seemed not to carry any meaning. Hating classes became a habit- not from rebellion but out of sheer disinterest.

Her school days were marked with an acute feeling of detachment. Most of the other children could hang onto something within the school life, be that friend, sports, or academic, but not Esa; she was average at best with her school work, barely enough to pass exams. As others bust themselves competing for good grades and recognition, the girl was trying to remain alive, counting down the days until the next exam, hoping she might just scrape through.

The school was meant to be a learning and growing place, but here, she drifted deeper into the belief of insecurity. Esa often ended up looking out of the classroom window, letting the world pass by. She wondered why she felt so out of place with others in the class. It was not loneliness from her aloofness; it felt much deeper than that. Rather, it was an invisible feeling that nobody seemed to care about her at all.

Recess was the toughest time of the day. While all the other kids were playing or sharing lunch in groups, she sat alone. No laughter and conversation could ever reach her ears. She gulped down her lunch so hastily that on occasions, she didn't have it at all, not even to shun sitting alone for too long. So she spends what seems like an eternity during these breaks looking out of a window, hiding in some corner until the bell rings again to carry them back into the classroom.

The challenge is that Esa did not have anyone to open up to, like most kids who have parents, siblings, or friends with whom to share their situation. She was as lonely at home as she was at school. No one asked her about her school day or comforted her through the school day's tough moments. The isolation that would envelop her was not one that was passed over; it was a reality that she faced.

It was not easy for Esa to tolerate this isolation as she grew older. She realised that her alienation from school was not just because she detested academics; it was deeper and emotional in nature. This derivational atmosphere at home bled into her school life, making it impossible for her to connect with people. No one had ever taught her how to connect with people; it sounded impossible to trust anyone when the family she belonged to seemed to have let her down in every step of life.

But deep inside, below the snarl of loneliness and disappointment, was a tiny spark of hope. Esa wanted something better. She couldn't put her finger on what it was, but she knew that this was not life, this hollow feeling; there had to be more. She just hadn't found it yet.

For the moment, though, Esa continued to drift through her school days, trying to make sense of a world that seemed determined to leave her behind. The existence was stiff and lonely, but deep inside, she held onto hope that someday things would change. Even if she did not know how she'd find a way out of the isolation that had defined her life for so long.

Esa had been to a "Subzi mandi" government school, where the teachers seemed to materialise, disappear, and materialise once again. However, for Esa, there was one constant. Mrs Kapoor's healthy, fair complexion made her stand out, with two missing front teeth, big spectacles that almost covered her face and a big mole on her left cheek. A smile robbed of; a tooth fairy having snatched them off. Every time the woman opened her mouth to say something, no one could help but focus on the "gate" between her teeth—it was like going into another dimension, an invitation to never-ending titters. Whenever she laughed her two lips went in opposite directions making it even funnier.

Then there was the hair. Oh, that middle part! So sharp it seemed as if her scalp was divided down the middle by a ruler, two straight, lifeless curtains framing her face. You could almost imagine the chalked-up drawing of an electrical current running down that part. Just her look would have been enough to make the students squirm in their seats, not bursting with laughter.

But her wardrobe? It was a completely different story. Mrs. Kapoor seemed to consider colours something of a blindfolded contestant in the game show. One day she would turn up in a bright neon green sari with a pink blouse so mismatched it looked as though Holi had exploded all over her. Her sense of fashion bore no consideration for coordination. Like, it was as if every morning she walked into her closet, twirled around three times, and pulled out what her hands first landed on. And oh, her laugh!

It wasn't some dainty, fragile giggle that a lady ought to have; it was something straight out of a Bollywood villain's playbook. It's like Gabbar Singh from *Sholay* except really turned up to the max volume. Every time Mrs. Kapoor laughed, it rang through the classroom as deep and booming, entirely out of place. Her laugh sent shivers down the spines of the poor little kids-not because it was spooky-but because it was impossible to take seriously. Poor little kids couldn't keep a straight face at the idea of her standing on a hillside, the wind blowing through her saree, letting out a manly, villainous roar. With missing teeth, a bizarre dress sense, and laughs that could run Gabbar to a stop, Mrs Kapoor was, without any doubts, the most eccentric and wittily funny and quaintly lovable teacher Esa would ever recall.

Esa, even as she had always managed to find ways out of most of the tough spots at school-especially parent-teacher-meeting time, again, to her dismay, was left completely to her own devices; since the one parent was gone, and the other rarely involved her in anything going on within their home. Her teachers long ago had grown accustomed to her falling grades, and Esa certainly knew that if her father ever showed up, everyone would see she wasn't doing a stellar job in school.

One day, in class, one of her teachers finally asked her about it. "Esa, where are your parents? They never come to parent-teacher meetings. Do they even know how you're doing in school?" the teacher raised an eyebrow as asking.

Esa felt her pancreas panicking rise to her chest, but she calmed down fast. "Well. You see, my mother doesn't stay with me," she said, voice overflowing with rehearsed sadness. The teacher's face softened with pity, and Esa knew that this was all she needed-it wasn't even that she missed her mother. But playing the sympathy card seemed like the best option.

"And your father?" the teacher pressed. "Why doesn't he come to the meetings?"

Esa stalled, knowing that the truth—that her father was too busy with work and wouldn't care much about her grades—would get her into even more hot water. So, she did what she always did in these situations: she lied.

"Oh. my dad. He's, uh, he's in Japan," she blurted out. The words were out of her mouth before she realised, she was thinking them, but once said, she was hooked.

"Japan?" The teacher blinked, looking thoroughly confused.

"Yes, Japan," Esa said, finding her courage. "He's on a business trip and won't be back till next week." She beamed innocently, hoping the teacher would drop it.

The teacher raised an eyebrow. "And what about your other relatives? Can't one of them come?"

Esa's mind was racing, but she wanted to keep this lie going. She said quickly, "Oh, they all live really far away. Like, other countries far."

The teacher sighed, clearly sceptical but still not sure of how to argue against the intricacy of Esa's story. Feeling the weight of her lie, she decided to sweeten the deal in a desperate attempt to sidestep more pointed questions. "But you know, I can ask my dad to bring you something from Japan when he gets back."

The teacher looked surprised. "What do you mean?"

"Well," Esa said, doing her best to look serious, "I can ask him to bring you a beautiful Japanese sari! You know, something unique, just for you."

She looked around with a quick-thinking face. "You know, you're my favourite teacher, and I begged my dad to get you the most beautiful one, just for you. You'll love it."

The room remained silent for a moment. The teacher stared at her, clearly trying to make sense of the ridiculous offer. "A. Japanese sari?" she repeated.

"Yes!" she nodded eagerly, already half-convinced of this fantastic lie. "They make the finest saris in Japan. You would love it."

The teacher was barely able to suppress a smile at this and clearly entertained the absurdity of the situation. "Okay, okay," she said with a waving motion of her hand, "We shall see when your father returns from Japan."

The relief that Esa felt was narrowly escaping disaster. She spent the rest of the day trying not to think about what would happen when the teacher found there were no saris in Japan and that her father was very much not on a business trip in a foreign country. Now, though, she had bought herself some time, and that was all that mattered.

For the next week, there was a shocking reversal of this attitude on the part of the teacher. She was nice to Esa, and she even made her class monitor for a week. Esa revelled in the reprieve from her usual troubles, but she knew this wouldn't last forever.

The weeks went by and the teacher's excitement over the mythical Japanese sari was slowly diffused, and once again, she focused on the real issue- Esa's father. "Okay," she said one day, "now it's time to bring your father to the next meeting. No more excuses."

In retrospect, the whole thing was ridiculous, and Esa used to laugh at how she thought about that day. She had invented wild stories to save herself from trouble, not for the first time in her life, and it was going to be the last such incident. Whether she said that all her relatives had died in tragic accidents or claimed business trips to distant lands, Esa had the art of deception perfected. It was her way of fighting back against this chaos in her life, her small act of rebellion against this world that wanted so much more from her than it could possibly give.

Years later, Esa would look back at her school days and laugh, incredulous at the lies she'd told. The tales she spun were so outlandish she couldn't help but wonder just how anybody ever believed her. But to her at the time, they had been her survival mechanism to carry on while everything around seemed to fall down.

But above all, perhaps, they had given her the much-needed release from the reality that she dreaded confronting.

Esa had always kept her way around complicated situations, especially when it involved her school as well as her teachers' expectations. She was not exactly a model student. Distracted most of the time, she didn't care much for academics. But there was something she excelled at: talking her way out of trouble. It was during one such episode that her teacher demanded to see her parents. It was not the first time this had occurred, and by now, Esa had developed a pretty good routine for getting out of it.

The third and fourth times, Esa ran out of stories again. She hadn't prepared her dad, but unwittingly, the school had been calling the landline at her grandma's house, where her father sometimes stayed. They had left a message, and before too long, her dad was in on the whole thing-the parent-teacher meeting.

No warning, Esa had built up a perfectly woven web of lies. She went to school the next day, assuming everything was normal. And there stood her father waiting for her outside the principal's office.

Her heart fell. The look in his eyes was neither angry nor upset, yet that disappointment in his face made her insides churn inside. He hadn't remembered the previous meetings she'd missed-or, worse, the tales she'd spun in a desperate attempt to keep him away-but now here he was, and there was no dodging the truth.

As she walked into the teacher's room beside him, Esa steeled herself for what was to come.

Esa knew the web of lies was on the verge of collapse the moment her father entered. She had evaded reality as long as she had by spinning enough tales to keep him from seeing what a mess she had become in school. Now, standing before her teacher and father, she felt exposed-to be herself was to be utterly naked.

He sat quietly, his lips sealed as the teacher began to speak. "How was your Japan trip?" the teacher asked with feigned casualness, dripping with annoyance. Esa's heart sinks. The lies she had spun out to keep her father at bay had buried that small fact so deep down that she forgot about it.

Her father frowned, clearly perplexed. "Japan trip?" he repeated, incredulous. "I never left Delhi in my life. What are you talking about?"

VERSES KINDLER PUBLICATION

The teacher wheeled around to Esa, her eyes squinting in a sort of combination of anger and disappointment. "Stand on one leg," she ordered, her voice cold. Esa's legs trembled as she complied, her face aflame with shame.

And then, as if she had been waiting for this moment, the teacher unleashed a torrent of complaints. "Your daughter is a mess! Every week, somebody in the family is either dead or else staying in the hospital. I have heard every excuse in the book from her! No studying, no improvement in her grades, and now this nonsense about Japan!"

The teacher was indignant now, saying, "Bend your knees, hold your ears, and act like a hen!" Esa retorted, "But how, ma'am? I am wearing a skirt, not feathers!" That did little to calm the irritation in Mrs. Kapoor's voice as she huffed, "Fine! Stand on one leg then!" Esa shrugged, and balanced on one leg, grumbling under her breath, "Guess I am a flamingo now."

Esa felt a small shrinking under the weight of her teacher's words. Her belly churned, and her eyes prickled with streams of tears, but she swallowed them all down. She had been in the habit of hiding her emotions, faking that nothing bothered her for as long as she could remember.

But then, she looked over at her father. The looks in his eyes would knock the wind out of someone. She had seen him angry before, but there was something so different about it now. It wasn't the frustration from a parent who could have expected better, but far deeper, far more personal.

The walk home was like a death march. She had tried to prepare herself for the impending scolding, but nothing could ever have prepared her for what was about to happen. As soon as they got home, her father exploded.

"You're a shame," he yelled. "You've brought nothing but shame to this family and nothing but trouble!" He towered above her, his fists clenched and his face red with rage. "Why was this child ever born to you? You are a curse like your mother. The whole family is cursed because of you!"

"You shouldn't have been born at all. I wish you were dead. Get out of this house! Go to hell, for all I care, but I do not want to be looking at your face again!"

Esa stood there, repeating the words in her head. She was breathless. It couldn't move even a millimeter. Always knew her father was unfair to her, but this was different. This was not discipline or frustration- this was rejection. Pure, unfiltered rejection. He wanted her gone. Wanted her dead.

There was pain, crushing pain that seemed to suck all that mattered below her feet and drop her like an earthquake right into the abyss. That is when something inside of her snapped. She realised that this one person whom she believed she could count on, whom she believed should protect her, didn't want her at all.

Without even thinking, she snatched up her little brother. He'd been sitting in the corner, wide-eyed with fear as he watched everything unfold. He didn't know what was happening, but he knew well enough to follow his sister.

"Come on," she whispered, her voice trembling. She didn't know where she was going, but she couldn't stay here now that her father had said what he just said.

They walked in silence to the bus stop. Esa didn't have a plan, but she had to get away. The words of her father kept ringing in her head like a poison seeping into her soul. "You're a curse... I wish you were dead."

They got on the first bus they saw, which was to Manali and all the places. Esa didn't care if it took her to Mars or anywhere else, as long as she got far removed from this house, she would never call home again. Her brother sat beside her, bewildered but trusting her completely.

The journey could have been out of a dream; the bus was on the highway, and the world going by outside the windows was nothing but an incoherent blur of shapes. However, inside Esa's mind was as sharp as a knife. She ran through her father's words - and with each repetition, felt the pain a little more acutely.

She had run from the truth for so long—lied to her teachers, hidden her pathetically low grades, and pretended everything was all right. But she could not run from this. She could no longer lie to herself. Her own father did not want anything to do with her.

She stayed for nine days' in Manali with her brother in her friend's house, who was studying with her in her school. Her friend's family took her in along with her brother and showered them with love. For the first time, she saw up close what a peaceful and loving family was like.

She was out of the world's sight, trying to think up plans for her future life. She was little more than a teenager, still not so very much a woman, and yet the weight of the world already rested on her shoulders.

She spent her days there, and she knew she was not going to stay there forever. She had to go back. Reaching back meant she would be seeing her father again, one thing she dreaded so much. What if he really meant it? What if he really did not want her anymore?

Those nine days taught Esa the painful truth: sometimes, those who are supposed to love and look out for you are the ones who hurt you the most. And no matter how hard it hurts; you must keep going.

Esa's days in Manali were like stepping into a world she'd never imagined existed. It had been nine days of such turmoil and suffering at home that those days were like a breeze to her.

She'd wake up in the morning to this friend's mom cooking breakfast in the kitchen. It's warm and envelopes her with such comfort compared with the biting, unyielding edges of her real life. No yelling or threats ever hung over their heads like a storm just about to break. Laughter and love seemed only to permeate the house. Her friend's father would come home from work, tired but smiling, with his children greeting and playing with him before having dinner with his wife. Together, they used to go to the market, pray at the church, and share ordinary happy moments that Esa never knew about.

For the first time, she lets herself believe that there really are families like that outside of the books she had read or TV shows. She was suddenly and shockingly made aware that not all homes are filled with fear, that not all fathers utter vile words to their children, and that mothers are capable of being there for their children rather than being far and away because of their situation.

She and her brother found solace in those days, a brief reprieve from the storm of their life back in Delhi. They laughed together and played with her friend's siblings, and for a while, they could almost pretend that they were part of this happy, loving family. They never thought about home, and Esa had convinced herself that her father would not care that they were gone. Indeed, hasn't he told her to leave? Hasn't he uttered those awful words which cut deeper into one's soul than a slap or a beating could ever do?

And Esa thought she would never ever leave Manali, living the inactivity of hiding away from all the harsh reality that waited for her back home in Delhi, intending not to come in touch with her father. She assumed he wouldn't even bother looking for her because, in the first place, he had made it clear how much he didn't want her around; what would make him care now if she was anywhere?

Well, of course, reality always has a way of catching up to you. After about nine days, her dad somehow found out where they were. This was Esa's first and last peaceful haven; when she saw him standing at the door of her friend's house, his face actually contorted with anger. Her stomach dipped down, and she knew what was coming.

He dragged her out of the house, angry, hardly giving her time to say a final goodbye to a family that had shown her what love could look like within a home, but her father's angry words lashed at her in sharp, snatching bursts as he condemned her for leaving the house, for running away. He was spitting mad, telling her that the police have been looking for her, that she causes havoc by disappearing that way.

She had ranted, full of frustration and anger: "You told me to leave, that we shouldn't have been born!" The other family saw the tension between the two and took pity on Esa. However, like so many Indian families do, they quietly and silently took the parents' side and swept the greater pain Esa had to bear under the rug.

And then came the beating. Right there in the street, with no one to care, he beat her. It was hurting in a different way, and his blows did not land heavy and hard but a myriad of words. He called her disgracing, burdening, and cursing. The peaceful days in Manali seemed to have disappeared like gone-gone rain with the drizzle as she stood there, hindering to hold back her tears, and was wont to allow him to see how much he had broken her again.

All was done. He pulled her and her brother back to the bus station. The ride back to Delhi was quiet- the weight of his disappointment and anger settling over them like a dark cloud. Esa stared out of the window with a heart filled with regret, knowing she could never run far enough to be able to really leave the life she was born into.

Life might be what Manali had shown her, but that is something too far-fetched. That reality is here, with the fact that he is a dad who made her life a curse and a life that gave no reprieve from all that tormenting heartache.

Chapter 5: Mentorship and Academic Transformation

Once the anger dissipated, though, Esa's father became wracked with guilt and fear for Esa's safety and his daughter's in the vast, unforgiving expanse of Delhi. He did not sleep nights; endless worry and a racing mind filled his days. Regret weighed heavy on the horse's soul.

But even now, she could hear the murmur of that bus grinding along the winding roads of Manali. Nine days away from Delhi, away from her father's fury, had gone deep into her mind. She was a teenager then, filled with rebellion, yet subduedly craving approval from the very man who had thrust her away.

Her father has always been quite strict and asked for much respect and obedience but was never really warm.

When Esa returned to Delhi, the home scenario did not change much. In typical Indian families, parental expectations are very rigid, and those expectations were not bent in Esa's case. Like most fathers, he envisioned a bright and predictable future for her. Whenever she asked Esa what she was doing or consulted her on matters, he would insist that she follow a straightforward profession or, as he called it, respected and stable. "What do you want me to become? " she would ask, only to hear his standard response: a doctor, engineer, or any other professional.

Between these new societal changes and the growing opportunities that existed beyond these traditional roles, her father held fast to his expectations, reflecting personal aspirations versus family pressures.

On hearing that, her father would often say to her, "I want you to become a doctor." She thought her life's path had been laid out, leaving no room for her desires or dreams. She hated it—hated the idea of being something she did not care about. Yet, she could never say that aloud. What would her father think? Or worse, what would he say?

The truth was, Esa never knew what she wanted to become. While other kids at school dreamt of becoming engineers, pilots, and lawyers, Esa floated through her childhood without an aim. School? That was another mess altogether. She wasn't bad with her studies but reckless. Esa's father had envisioned her taking up a profession that symbolized prestige and success in his eyes. For Esa, however, the white coat and syringe did not even spark excitement within her. It was another far cry from uncertain dreams. Her father never hid his hope that she should follow in the footsteps of other students of medicine. He has always pressed her to pursue science, which felt all the more oppressive against this backdrop of other children in the family receiving extra support in the form of private tutors and special coaching. Although her father's wealth was never in question, emotional and practical support was woefully lacking. Esa barely passed through her tenth grade with mere passing marks. Her academic performance reflected her disconnection from a path she never chose.

The pressure to become a dream of her father became overwhelming, and she went on to navigate through a future that she had never imagined for herself: barely keeping up academically. Esa, to this day, bears the constant burden of her dad's expectations pressing against her. He always wanted her to become a doctor, but it wasn't her dream. Her father was keen that she do science after 10th grade because he wanted to pursue his ambitions for her. The pressure to perform was one thing, but it was the constant comparison with other children in the extended family that hurt.

The cousins were sent to tuition and private tutors came into their house, and their study journey seemed effortless compared to hers. Esa's father had always provided for her. She knew it was not about money; it was about the broken family dynamics. Esa often would wonder, "What is the good of the money you make if you don't spend it on the well-being of your own child?"

In her case, her father had been emotionally absent creating a gap that no material wealth could fill in. However, all the other children in the family seemed to have it all. Their parents were those who were actively interested and came forward as helpers, proving proactive about their education making sure they had every advantage to succeed. And the comparisons were relentless. The relatives would come around at family gatherings and proudly talk of their children's academic successes, relating story after story of how their sons and daughters were succeeding in the more competitive tuitions and coaching schools.

She was invisible in these conversations like she didn't matter, as if she was not worthy because she was not up to the high standards she was supposed to meet. Her father would point at her cousins, who were thriving, and tell her why she could not be like them. This continuous comparison made her feel she was not good enough, no matter how hard she tried. It wasn't just school-related; it turned into a question of self-worth where her grades and how she performed compared to that of her cousins mattered. With every passing day, loneliness acquires deeper wounds.

The broken family dynamics did not help much as well. She did not get emotional support from her father; neither was she able to get practical support from him. Though she spent some time with him, emotionally as well as practically, for the benefit of her father, it did not matter to her because Esa's emotional and practical support then, was missing in his life. All these comparisons weighed on her, creating a deep sense of resentment. She started thinking about what made her father not invest in her education like all other parents would for their children. If they have the money, then why wasn't that money used to try to make sure she succeeds? But it was more than just academic support she needed; she yearned for the emotional support that all those other kids seemed to get so easily.

Their parents were engaged, and that made all the difference.

He never realized what it was that she needed more than anything.

He never understood it was his encouragement and belief in her potential that went missing. Esa's journey through schooling ended feeling deserted. The father became angry with her. It was the day she flunked her 11th-grade exams - disaster. Esa was not even shocked. She had never liked science anyway, but her father had insisted on it, so that meant a predictable failure. He was shocked when he heard that his daughter had flunked class 11. Esa was hopeful in his eyes about becoming a doctor, and the only thing that mattered to him was fetching his daughter a successful and secure future.

He was smashed by this news like a storm with shock, disappointment, and a deep sense of failure as a parent.

He never could have thought that things would go so badly wrong. He had forced his daughter into science against all her wishes. Not good enough.

For him, it was a professional failure, a blow to the dream he had woven for her future.

To him, it was something personal, a shame for the family. He could not understand the situation whereby his daughter-who was meant to be a doctor failed. "Do you know what people will say?" he shouted at her. "How will I face my family? You're a shame, Esa. You're no better than your mother. A curse, both of you." Those words had cut deep, slicing through whatever confidence Esa had left. She couldn't bear the weight of his disappointment. But it wasn't just disappointment—his words were cruel, a type of hurt that dug into her soul. Esa, on the other hand, had never truly wanted to pursue science.

She had compromised her own interests and desires, trying to fit into a mould that wasn't hers. His pressure on her and the constant comparisons with other children in the family had left her feeling overwhelmed and disconnected from her passions. It wasn't as if she wasn't cut out for class 11 material but because they pushed her into a stream of her choice without any interest from her side. Parents, often because of societal expectations and their very own unfulfilled dreams, also push their children into careers that they find stable or glamorous. However, this often also leads to disengagement, stress, and ultimately even failure. When they are compelled to take routes where they do not even come close to enjoying what they do, they are cheated of the excitement of learning or discovering themselves and get lost, like Esa. Moreover, Esa's father made another decision that left her without power: he decided to move back to her grandmother's house, which was full of mournful memories for her. For Esa, it felt like going back to hell, a place where her inconsiderate circumstances seemed to lurk inside her head.

The house was suffocating, and with every step inside, the weight of the past traumas and pains made themselves known. But she never had control over it. Her father's choices ruled her life, and she and her brother were to return to this prison, that house. Deep down, Esa was scared and angry, but by 11th grade, something inside of her had shifted. The failure of her previous year and the demands to play out a path she never wanted had bred a quiet but determined resolve in her.

She finally gathered the courage to tell her dad, "Listen, I do not want to be a doctor." It was a big step for her in this regard, but the reply came straight from his dismissal.

He said, "At least let us see you finish your graduation.". Or if not, leave after passing your 12th, get married and leave. His words kill her soul by putting before her two cages: academic achievement or marriage. Life continued, but it was never quite the same. The burden of failure, academic and emotional, hung over Esa like a dark cloud. She knew she couldn't go back to the way things had been. She had to find something—some purpose, some path that belonged to her and not to her father's dreams or to the expectations of her family. The family in Esa's grandmother's house was quite strange. They were always very hospitable, always receiving outsiders because of kindness and hospitality to guests or distant acquaintances. However, this had never been shown to their family members. And so, there was a sense of detachment, coldness, and even resentment in the family.

Esa felt that it was as if the house had invisible walls between them emotionally.

Their values appear to be more in the interest of appearances to outsiders than creating much of an inner bond. It was a place where duty and reputation mattered way more than genuine connection and care. That's when Shukla Uncle joined her mainstream. He was never a member of the family; he just stayed in the same house as her uncle. But there was something different about this man. In comparison to her father, Shukla Uncle did not shoo her into a career that she did not want. Instead, he recognised her potential and not her failures. Mr. Shukla's words went straight to the heart of Esa's mind.

The day he asked her such a simple and profound question, "If you want to go to heaven, what do you have to do?" in such simple words that she felt caught off guard. She said, "Well, probably being good and doing the right things will get me there."

To gain heaven, you must first die," he said with a smile. "Are you ready for that?" Metaphorical words were enough for Esa to know that if she wanted to change the life she had lived up to that point, she would have to let go of her past and stand up to some tough issues.

He guided her, gave her wisdom and support, and helped her see what lay ahead.

If you want to change your life, you have to start now, Shukla uncle had told her one day, after yet another argument with her father about her future. 'Can't wait for others to hand you the answers. You have to find them yourself,' he would say. This was the first time Esa had been spoken to as if it were believed that she could actually learn and that everything was indeed possible. He started coaching her and took her through her studies, and Esa slowly began seeing herself in a light that she had never had before. For the first time, she wasn't the reckless backbencher barely managing to make it. She was able, smart, and had a future that she could decide on. The next two years would see a complete change in Esa. She would devote herself to studying: hours with Shukla Uncle, solving problems and learning to appreciate the value of education. And it paid. She had once failed. Suddenly, she topped her class in the 11th standard, which was nothing short of shocking to all. The teachers, students, and even her family were left stunned, aghast by this dramatic turnaround. Whispers around the street-what is it that the one who failed times before now to stand on top?

Some of them doubt her capabilities and feel that there must have been some fact misplaced; unable to believe it is the same girl.

In Esa, on the other hand, there was a significant element of validation and overwhelming.

It was proof that no matter the seeming stories, given how things used to seem about anyone's story, with pure effort and determination, it can be rewritten and told in any manner needed.

When Esa topped her class, her eyes sparkled with pride. It wasn't very often that she had seen her father smile so visibly, but her heart swelled to see him do so now. He took her to Palika Bazaar, their usual place for small celebrations, but today was different. As they entered the market, which was teeming with life, he turned back to her and, with a smile that said it all, "Buy whatever you want- five-ten, as many things as you like." Then he settled down on a small stool near the shop's entrance, giving her full liberty to indulge without his usual careful glances or suggestions.

This was not just any shopping spree for Esa. She knew her father too well-he did not say much, but the man within him was always full of emotions. He'd take her to the markets whenever he was visibly happy. Janpath and Palika Bazaar became their little sanctums, places where he'd show joy without saying much. She could always feel the warmth in his silence, the pride hidden beneath his quiet demeanour. These journeys were like festivals to her - as though the mundane markets lit up Diwali's own magic.

As she wandered through the aisles, picking up a few clothes and trinkets, she couldn't help but steal a glance back. There he sat, patiently watching her. His was a contented smile, not because of what she bought but by knowing he had made her feel special. It wasn't ever about the things that never were; it was about those moments when she felt like his whole world, and today, that world was a little brighter.

She topped again when she was in the 12th grade. It was a complete turnaround from the girl who had flunked just a couple of years before.

But even then, her father wasn't satisfied. "Become a civil servant," he urged her. "Get a government job. That's the only secure future."

But little did the family know Esa had other plans. She wanted to study mass communication, tell stories, to be a journalist. Her father, influenced by his family, couldn't understand why she would choose such an unstable career. "A girl in mass communication?" they scoffed. "What kind of job is that for a respectable family?"

Still, Esa persisted. If there was one thing she had discovered in the past few years, she did not need to ask for permission to live her dreams. And with Shukla Uncle's encouragement, she applied to colleges, got a good one, and embarked on a new journey.

It wasn't easy. Obstacles were still there, still moments of doubt. But Esa was no longer the lost, reckless child she was once considered. She had found her way, not through her father's expectations but her own determination.

Esa was always an independent-minded person, but her desire to pursue a career in mass communication came face to face with the orthodox views of her family. Her father, along with other relatives, insisted that she prepare for government jobs or civil services, which was the ultimate stamp of success in their minds. In their eyes, a government job was one of the safest and most prestigious options, while Esa always used to be a rebel, refusing to give in to these expectations.

She had hopes that the father would welcome the idea of having a journalist in the family. She saw the twinkle in his eyes as he thought her daughter would be doing something that no one had done in the family. However, the refusal came swiftly and without warning. It hurt her heart, not a simple "no" really but layered with tradition, family, and old belief systems. She thought so much of her father, and deep within her, she knew he wasn't at all rigid or close-minded. The refusal was not entirely his.

Her mind drifted back to a tale he had narrated to her a few times. It was a slice of his life that always brightened his face with a mix of nostalgia and regret. When young, her father had harbored ambitions to be an actor. He had been a great fan of the embers of the great Rajesh Khanna, the superstar who had dominated the silver screen. In reality, that dream had burned so bright within him that he once ran off from their home in Delhi, to Mumbai by train, on nothing but hopes and stars in the eyes, to be like Khanna, and to live that life of glamour and passion.

That dream didn't last for long. Her grandfather, furious and embarrassed by his son's defiance, tracked him down and brought him back. Their family was extremely conservative and traditional; they never believed in such professions. Acting like so many other creative jobs was considered a lowly job. It wasn't held in their light as "respectable" or "honorable." Her father had to give up on that dream, and life moved on, though Esa knew a part of him never truly let go of it.

Sitting there, she couldn't help but think that her father refused her because that was the same thing he feared. He was not saying no to her dream because he wasn't believing it-he was because he, too, was trapped in the beliefs of their family. A family where professions like journalism were dangerous and almost dishonourable, especially for a woman. As soon as the father had confided his decision to the relatives, they had flooded his head with usual cautions - "Journalists wear short dresses, they stay out late, they mix with the wrong crowd. Not for a respectable girl."

And that had been enough to make him change his mind. Her father, who once dared to chase his dream in acting, had become a victim of the same pressure that crushed his ambitions. Esa understood, though the bitterness still gnawed at her. She knew, deep down inside, that her father may have supported her if not for the old-fashioned ideas emanating from the family.

The real tragedy, she thought, wasn't the refusal of her dream but rather reflected the suppressed dreams of her father. She saw it in his eyes-the silent apology that lingers there every time he says no to her. He didn't want her to feel the same pain he felt but could not break free from the grip of family expectations. And so, Esa was stuck between the urge to keep on pursuing her passion and with tradition looming over to invade her father's life and now hers.

When the mass communication option got blocked, she switched to the other side and asked her father to allow her to pursue law (LLB). She was surprised when he became optimistic about her since she had handled her previous grades, 10th, 11th and 12th pretty decently, though her initial few years didn't work much out. Nonetheless, despite his understanding of her abilities, the father was again influenced by the rest of the family members, who constantly crumpled him down to decide for her.

Esa's father always assumed she'd be a great doctor one day, always dismissing playful protests by saying, "I'd be a terrible one! " He says that though, with her steady hand in giving him injections for his diabetes, this was proof enough. He bragged about her potential to everyone, but his tender heart was also well-tutored by family pressures. When Esa decided to become a journalist, he was never able to back her, simply held back by conservative views. She wished he had supported her to achieve that. She wanted parents to know that standing behind their children and, in particular, whenever they believe in what they are following would be very significant in growing and being happy.

Determined to move forward, Esa chose to pursue higher education and filled out applications to some of India's top colleges. She indeed studied hard, but she failed in gaining admission to the elite institutions, like Hindu College or St Stephen's, for which she had always had a keen eye. She eventually got admitted to Janki Devi Memorial College, Jesus and Mary College, where she earned history honors.

Despite staying with all sorts of family members, Esa felt she was the lousiest daughter nobody has ever had. She was unhappy. It was then that there chanced to come a gentleman, Shukla, who, noticing Esa, inquired about what or rather whom was troubling her. She spoke of her apprehensions and reiterated her desire to pursue BCA, though her heart didn't lie in it. The journey that began in 2004-2005 was very crammed with struggles, which made Esa the person she is. She kept fighting in order to chart her own path and not follow the pattern that society had laid before her, alongside the expectations of her family. And so it was that she sat in her dorm room at college all those years later, reflecting on everything that had brought her to this time and to this place. It dawned on her an important thing: this journey wasn't about proving anything to her father; it was about proving to herself that she could go above the chaos that filled her life, above the brokenness of her family, and build something beautiful in life.

VERSES KINDLER PUBLICATION

Chapter 6: Love, Loss, and Resilience

Esa never would have guessed that she would meet the guy who would, for a while, rule her entire universe by coincidence in the busy metropolis of Delhi. He was a Dehraduni man named Patrick who worked in Delhi. There was a certain something about them from the first minute they met. Even though Esa was naturally rebellious, she had always hidden a romantic side from the world.

Patrick was a man who radiated a calm assurance that drew others to him with ease. His lofty stature was emphasized by his impeccably cut attire, which exuded a certain elegance in his demeanour. His gentle, deep-set eyes gave off the impression that they could see past appearances and into a person's inner world. His soft smile exuded warmth and generosity, and his well-groomed dark hair and light stubble on his jawline gave him an image of maturity. He spoke in a way that made everyone feel important and always opened doors and pulled out chairs with the grace of a gentleman.

It wasn't just Patrick's appearance that attracted Esa; it was his virtues. He was patient, never pressuring her to accept his viewpoints or make snap decisions. She felt heard in a manner that no one else had because he listened to her with true curiosity. His composure, even when they disagreed, was a far cry from the turmoil in her history. He often spoke about creating a stable future and had a strong work ethic and steadfast sense of duty. Esa felt protected, seen, and loved because of his ambition, nurturing demeanour, and respect for her aspirations.

Through mutual friends, they had first connected, and their friendship quickly developed into something intense and all-consuming. As Patrick had a certain charm, a quiet strength about him that pulled her in. He was simple, grounded, and yet deeply ambitious. These qualities made her feel both secure and excited about a future with him. His Christian upbringing in a small village didn't initially bother Esa, whose own mother was Christian. In fact, that common ground seemed to offer a sense of familiarity.

Their first few dates seemed like stuff from a fantasy. They would talk about their goals, their love of travelling, and most importantly, their futures, for hours on end. They spoke about marriage as if it was inevitable, and in Esa's mind, it was. She could see herself with Patrick forever. For once, she felt safe and hopeful, certain that she had found someone who would support her through the storms of life.

They plotted, planned their marriage, and dreamed of their future together. Patrick assured her that she would lead a happy life that was very different from the hardships she had experienced as a child. It appeared as nothing could go wrong for a while.

However, reality quickly collapsed, just like everything else in life does. Patrick was raised in a traditional Christian home that respected customs and strictly followed the norms of his community. His mother, a woman who wielded significant influence in his life, was not particularly fond of Esa from the beginning. She had her own ideas about what kind of girl her son should marry, and to her, Esa simply didn't fit the mould.

Initially, Esa was hopeful that things would smooth over, and that Patrick's family would eventually accept her. She met them, trying her best to be polite and open. However, the first few meetings were cold and awkward. Patrick's mother scrutinized her every move, finding faults wherever she could. Esa tried to keep her spirits up, but every interaction chipped away at her confidence.

The breaking point came when Patrick's mother summoned Esa for a serious conversation. Her tone was stern and unforgiving. "You will need to convert to Christianity, fully. No half measures," she said bluntly, her eyes fixed on Esa. "And this city life—it has no place in your future. You will come and live with us in Dehradun, in the village, away from all these distractions. Your job, your independence—it all ends. You will be a full-time wife. A proper woman does not need a career to define her. Your focus will be the family, the household."

Esa sat there, stunned. The earth beneath her feet seemed to have vanished. She had put in a great deal of effort to become independent and develop a unique identity. Her work served as more than simply a source of income; it was a representation of her independence, self-worth, and capacity for self-sufficiency. It was oppressive to consider losing everything and being forced to live a life she didn't choose. She looked at Patrick, expecting him to offer some encouragement, but he said nothing, not wanting to confront his mother. Esa realized at that moment that she would have to sacrifice everything she had fought for—her independence, her dreams, her identity—if she stayed.

Esa's heart sank. It wasn't just about religion; it was about control, about the life Patrick's mother envisioned for her. A life in which Esa would lose her individuality, her independence, and her goals. She always dreamed of an ambitious life, but instead, she would end up a housewife in a small village, expected to live up to strict social norms.

As if the demands to give up her career and convert weren't enough, Patrick's mother took the conversation to an even darker place. She leaned forward, her voice cold and full of judgment. "And let's not forget," she said, eyeing Esa critically, "you come from a broken family. A girl raised without proper structure, without proper values. What kind of home can you hope to build? There's always an issue with girls from homes like yours. Healing doesn't come easily, and wounds like yours... they run deep."

Esa felt a sharp sting at her words, but before she could respond, Patrick's mother continued, her voice laced with cruelty. "Your mother... what kind of woman raises a child like you? She clearly failed in her duties. She couldn't even hold her family together. How could I ever accept a girl from such a dysfunctional home? Do you really think I'd allow my son to marry into that mess?"

As the onslaught of her family progressed, her heart hammered in her chest. It hurt to hear someone else disparage her in this manner. Despite her flaws, her mother remained her mother. The venom in Patrick's mother's words cut deeper than she expected. She looked at Patrick, hoping he'd step in, but his silence was deafening, a betrayal she could never forget.

These words felt like knives in Esa's heart. Even though she didn't get along well with her own mother, she found it horribly intolerable when Patrick's mother disparaged her mother and her family. She turned to face Patrick in the hopes that he would protect her from his mother's critical remarks. But all she saw was his silence. He shifted uncomfortably but said nothing, offering no support.

That silence spoke volumes. That's when Esa understood that the man she had planned a future with, the man she thought would always be at her side, was not strong enough to stand up for her when it really mattered. She was deeply in love with him, but when disappointment and treachery crept in, it started to fall apart.

Esa left that meeting with a heavy heart. She was angry, not just at Patrick's mother but at Patrick himself. How could he let his mother say such things about her? About her family? He had known everything—her struggles, her pain, her past—yet he had stood by while his mother tore her down.

In the days that followed, Patrick tried to reach out, apologizing and pleading for her to understand. "I'll talk to her again," he said. "I'll make her understand. I love you, Esa." But Esa had heard enough.

His failure to stand up for her in that crucial moment had broken something inside her, something that could never be repaired.

"I loved you," she said one evening, her voice trembling with emotion, "but love isn't enough when you can't even fight for me. Your mother disrespected me and my family, and you stood there, silent. I can't live my life with someone who doesn't value me enough to take a stand."

Patrick tried to argue, but Esa's mind was made up. With a heavy heart, she ended the relationship. It was painful, more painful than she could have ever imagined, but it was necessary. She knew that staying with him, compromising her identity and dreams, would have destroyed her in the long run.

The breakup left Esa shattered, but it also ignited a fire in her. For the first time in her life, she realized the true value of self-respect and independence. She learned that love, no matter how intense, is not enough if it comes at the cost of losing oneself. In Patrick's silence, she had discovered her own voice. In his failure to defend her, she found the strength to stand up for herself.

Her healing journey wasn't easy. In the days after the breakup, Esa felt lost. She threw herself into her work and studies, trying to drown out the pain. But as time passed, she began to understand the lessons the relationship had taught her.

She discovered that genuine love is based on respect for one another and being with someone who is there for you through good times and bad. She discovered that a partnership based on identity and moral compromise can never be genuinely successful. Above all, she understood that happiness had to originate from within herself and could not be obtained from anybody else.

Esa also came to appreciate the importance of family, even with all its complexities. After the breakup, she told her mother about everything, expecting judgment or disappointment. Esa's mother, despite their complicated relationship, provided her with a sense of solace when she needed it the most. She held Esa gently and spoke with unwavering calmness, "It's okay, beta. Life doesn't end with one heartbreak. You deserve someone who truly loves and respects you for who you are. Don't ever think you need to compromise or settle for less. You're strong, and there's so much ahead for you." Her mother's words, though simple, carried a weight of wisdom, reminding Esa that she was worthy of love that didn't come with conditions or judgments.

That support meant the world to Esa. It served as a reminder that, in the end, her family would always support her, regardless of their previous difficulties.

Through this traumatic event, Esa developed into a stronger, more confident woman. She realized that she could follow her own goals and aspirations without anyone else's approval, so she started concentrating more on them. She put all of her efforts into her studies, finished her degree, and set out on a road that would ultimately take her to a successful career.

In retrospect, Esa saw that despite their difficult relationship, it had been a significant turning point in her life. She had learned the virtues of independence, self-worth, and the strength of standing up for her convictions. She knew then that she was prepared for whatever lay ahead in life.

Esa and Patrick's relationship was a tale of development as much as love and heartache. She had come to trust herself above all else through the highs and lows, the happiness and the suffering. She had been shaped by the experience, which had enabled her to assert her individuality and convictions.

Esa had lost the love she had once believed would last forever, but she had come out stronger, smarter, and more self-reliant than before. For the rest of her life, the lessons she had learnt will help her make decisions and form connections.

And while Esa would always be reminded of Patrick and the pain he brought about, she was aware that she had improved as a result. She had learned that self-love is the foundation of true love and that no relationship is worth compromising your identity and pleasure for.

Esa had several emotional highs and lows during her protracted healing process. She was absolutely broken after the traumatic split—judged harshly by his family, abandoned by someone she had loved profoundly, and forced to doubt her own value. She spent weeks trying to come to terms with the breakup, frequently feeling overtaken by the feelings triggered by the harsh remarks about her family history. Not only did the split signal the end of a relationship, but it also reminded her of her own hardships as a youngster and the profound fears she carried with her.

Esa retreated into herself at first, but she gradually started to put her life back together. She set herself to work, concentrating on both her professional and personal objectives. It turned into a means of her taking back control of her life and reminding herself that she was resilient no matter what other people thought of her. She found purpose in her work, and she experienced a resurgence of self-worth with every little triumph. Esa discovered individuals who saw her for who she really was—not as someone defined by her family's past or her failed relationship, but as a capable, creative woman with a bright future ahead of her—by surrounding herself with supportive friends and coworkers.

Her insight also played a critical role in her healing. She could now address the long-standing problems that had surfaced throughout her relationship with Patrick. She gave herself permission to face her past and, more significantly, to accept that her future was not defined by her family's past. She discovered that she was capable of ending the vicious cycle of suffering and dysfunction and that she was deserving of unconditional love, free from outside criticism.

As the months passed, Esa began to embrace her newfound independence. She started exploring hobbies she had long neglected, finding solace in simple joys. She started practicing self-care, which helped her rediscover who she was and restore her confidence. Over time, the hurt of the split subsided and was replaced by a greater awareness of her own power. She came to the realization that she could feel worthy without anyone's approval. Her worth sprang from within and wasn't based on a relationship or other people's opinions.

Ultimately, the encounter imparted to her one of the most significant truths in life: genuine recovery arises from embracing and cherishing oneself, rather than seeking approval from others. And Esa discovered a power she didn't know she possessed in that self-love.

Chapter 7: Breaking Away: Career Beginnings and Independence

Independent by nature, not much comes easy. Challenges, fears, and unexpected turns require much growth in ways people never imagined. For this protagonist, independence meant being free from the shackles of the family her, society her, and perhaps most importantly, from herself- not getting away from home or earning one's own pocket money. This chapter marks the beginning of her quest for that freedom, a journey that takes her from a small town in India to the busy international city of Dubai, teaching her along the way resilience, courage, and the discovery of self.

The first step toward independence was when Esa chose to join NIFT, a choice which laid the template for her professional career and marked the first instance of her defiance of her family's wishes. Her family valued conventional careers: government jobs and civil services. She was an in-revolt child from a pretty young age, not interested in the norm set for her by her family and particularly her father. It was a different passion she harboured; her fascination with technology led to an overwhelming interest in what could be done in the digital world and how far one might be able to push oneself in this rapidly expanding field.

With her first admission to pursue a BCA soon followed, she was relieved pressures that had been built around her finally eased out. And it seemed like a victory. All the pressures that were built around her didn't come easy. Not everything is supported in her family. Her family hated the thought of her studying whatever she wanted, whereas her father resignedly relented but the rest of the family saw it as a deviation from what a woman was meant to be in their household. She could do no more to try or plead as the pressure to get back on course was very overwhelming, yet she stuck to her decision.

Her experience studying at a girls' college with BCA has been an odd one for her. She never felt less lonely in her life with the phenomenal people surrounding her. There were instances when loneliness seemed to overwhelm her every waking minute, but she never let that happen. She alone handled everything, from taking time to fill up forms to finding her way through the demanding world of higher education - all by herself and feeling entirely unsupported by those she had grown up among. This was a lesson of suffering and a learning experience for her. She was taught isolation, solitude, and self-reliance, all the while listening to her instincts, no matter what anybody had to say about her.

It is during her college years that she finds this mentor-her Shukla Uncle, through this distant relative who seems to think that she has something good that many in her family may not see. He made her take that kind of decision when she joined NIFT and then secretly supported her in making an application for a BCA. It was through his quiet guidance that she began to believe in herself and started taking those first steps towards a career. Within six months, she secured an internship where she learned C++, Java, and other programming languages. This was a step she felt would turn out to be crucial as it eventually brought her to join a computer course.

This professional course proved to be a landmark in every respect in her professional life, for at 22 years of age, she was the youngest faculty on her roll teaching programming languages to eager students, some of whom were older than she was. It wasn't easy. Questions were raised about her ability to teach at such a young age, and even if she had enough experience handling such responsibility. She continued her education and her hard work twice more to prove that capability is not deterred by age.

For the first time in her life, she was earning her pocket money, a handsome amount of ₹15,000/- per month which was significantly higher than many of her cousins working in a government service. The new financial independence came as a shock to her family, especially her father, who never made an effort to understand her and what career he wanted for her. For her, though, it was much more than money. It was that first, tangible proof that she had made the right decision, that following her heart led her to success, and that she did not need her family's approval to find success in her life.

Though her professional life flourished, it was unravelling in her personal life. Her health then was severely compromised by alcoholism, diabetes, and heart conditions at worst; and her father's health began to deteriorate rapidly. The burden of responsibility indeed fell squarely on her shoulders when her father suffered his first heart attack. During the height of the crisis, her family turned against her, accusing her of having caused her father's condition through her independence and career aspirations. She had stood there in the hospital, grasping her little brother's hand, with such a sense of helplessness that she could not do any more absolutely, turned inside out as she was. And those who hadn't been able to bear to help her when she needed them heaped blame upon her and asked her to work to mend what was broken.

Her connection with her father had been complicated. This was a man torn between his love for his children and his loyalty to his extended family, which had always had such a strong hold on him. He had never stood up to his elder brother or the rest of the family, a passivity that had deeply hurt her. Though he was always generous and good to his family, the children suffered from neglect, especially during his later years when his health was almost gone.

It's worth noting that at the end, just before he died, there was a small reconciliation period when her father started reconnecting with her mother, who had been in cold turkey for all those years. There was a small glimmer of hope for some brief period that the family might once again come together. However, such hopes were soon to be vanquished. On the very day when her mother was due to come back home, a father was struck by a powerful heart attack and left the family in utter shock. It was 4:30 AM, and it was at this moment, like a thunderbolt, that all the dreams of family unity were shattered in her mind. He had died just after taking a shower, on his way to the hospital.

What ensued was a time of great grief, not only over her father but also realising that her family, already fractured, had totally broken up. The extended relatives who were once part of her life cut all ties with them after he died. No visits were ever made, not even phone calls from the cousins that she was brought up with. It was as though they did not exist in their world. To make matters worse, they soon realized that her father had left behind a huge debt. Strangers would come knocking at their front door, searching for loans that could not be paid for, threats about loan proceedings, and claims they were never privy to.

Through the midst of all these, she was having a fight with her mother. She had always held a grudge against her mother who left the family when they were young. Their communication had never been good, barely any interaction at all. But six or seven months after her father's death, something was different. One day, tears fell from her mother's eyes, and she folded her hands in a gesture of apology and told her the truth about how she suffered abuse from her father's side of the family.

The stories her mother shared were horrifying. She had been imprisoned and denied food, and even attempts had been made to assassinate her when she was pregnant. All those revelations shattered the image that she had held of her mother all these years. Gradually, they began rebuilding their relationship. Her mother showed her old letters she had written, photos, and even made homemade jewellery kept for her. For the first time in her life, she started realizing she was not seeing her mother as the woman who had walked out on them but rather a woman who had experienced unimaginable suffering and yet survived.

The healing time closer them together, while the scars of the past remained. Her mom, now both parent and confidant, was a source of strength as she transitioned through these complexities and now went on to deal with loss, instability financially, and personal growth.

Her professional life was still progressing, though. She had spent years in NIIT and was now deciding whether to go further. The software industry was rich and rewarding but no longer the right place for her. It was such a comfortable place for her to be in but increasingly becoming stagnant with comfort. She yearned for more - a new challenge. She wanted something challenging, something that would test her boundaries beyond what she could boast of so far.

An opportunity came in the shape of a job offer in the banking sector, though a very different field requiring a new set of skills and a new frame of thinking. It wasn't easy for her to make that transition. The world of banking was much stiffer in its dealing as compared to the world she had moved out of. The stakes were higher, the pressure much more intense, and the steepness of the learning curve threatened to overwhelm her. She had to learn quickly, adopting financial systems and processes that at first would be foreign to her.

She often found herself wondering in the early stages whether she made the right move. Failure was always an option, and so was the challenge of proving themselves in a male-dominated industry where women were set aside. With every challenge though came an opportunity for growth. Her analytical abilities were trained through years of programming, and thus she could easily and sometimes very comfortably deal with the most complex financial data presented before her, while as a teacher, it helped her relay intricate concepts to clients and colleagues.

Yet, in the new world, she discovered her groove. She learned more about herself, her strengths, how to adjust, and what it takes to thrive in unfamiliar waters outside of this beautiful accomplishment in the banking business.

Banking was yet another leap towards independence with all the struggles and triumphs bundled with the experience.

Esa had always dreamed of working in Dubai, and when an opportunity finally presented itself through a friend, she was determined to make it happen despite the odds stacked against her. With only 30,000 in savings and no financial support from her family, every step felt like an uphill battle. The journey to Dubai for the interview was grueling; she had to stretch every rupee, questioning whether this gamble would be worth it. She endured the process with hope, but after the interview, weeks passed with no sign of the offer letter she had anticipated. Disappointment washed over her as she returned to India, heartbroken and feeling like her chance had slipped away.

Back home, Esa couldn't shake the feeling of failure. Her dream of working abroad seemed further out of reach than ever. But just as she was starting to lose hope, a friend called and urged her to check her junk folder for any missed emails. Filled with anxiety, Esa hesitated—could she really have overlooked something so important? She opened her email and nervously navigated to the spam folder.

There it was. The elusive email from the bank, offering her the position in the banking sector. Relief and excitement flooded over her, but the experience had left her emotionally exhausted. The delay had not only tested her patience but also shaken her confidence, making her question everything. Yet now, with the offer in hand, Esa felt a renewed sense of purpose, realizing that sometimes the road to success is paved with unexpected hurdles.

When her experience in banking continued for the rest of her life, another opportunity came by.

She would eventually take this step and migrate to a new country, far from everything familiar, for this job in Dubai. So much more different from the small town in India where she had grown up, Dubai with its skyscrapers sprawling onto the sky and fast-paced lifestyle. So it opened windows of new opportunities for her but forced her to leave all the support she had built over time.

The move to Dubai was exciting, yet nerve-racking. Cultural shocks of staggering dimensions began to set in and made adjusting a very difficult task for her. She was planted in an environment, after which she had to grapple with the subtleties of a new work culture diverse population from all other parts of the world. It was like again being a novice.

The early days were not that easy. She had the weight of proving herself: finding her place in a city known for its competitiveness. There were moments when she doubted herself; she'd wonder if she had made the right decision by leaving behind what she knew in India to drive into uncertainty in Dubai. She worked through it again.

Slowly, she got a hold of herself. Dubai's cosmopolitan streets offered her opportunities that no one at home would have ever imagined. The city could not but force her to quickly grow accustomed to its culture and lifestyle. It taught her to navigate the underlying intricacies of the workplace, how to assert herself in a competitive environment, and how to accept the diverseness that living in such a global metropolis bestowed on her.

Underpinning this journey was the emotional curve of defining her growth as a human being. The thrill of promising opportunities was always to be balanced with fear and dread. All the decisions she made—her stepping into a new industry, her beginning anew in a new country, or rebuilding her relationship with her mother—all carried different doses of emotions together: fear, doubts, excitement, and determination to bring her forward to who she became.

In these surroundings, one thing remained the same: her will to succeed. Independence, she found, didn't necessarily mean moving out of home and making money. It means taking control of your life, making decisions that reflect on what you value as a person, and getting strength out of difficulty. It is learning how to accept, as true, the complexities of relationships, and living within their thin lines as the body selflessly serves its spirit.

VERSES KINDLER PUBLICATION

The road to independence was far from over; despite everything she had been through, challenges were still ahead, obstacles to overcome, and lessons to be learned. Yet with each step forward, she became stronger, more resilient, and determined to pave her own road in life.

Chapter 8: The Return of Past Demons

Esa's career path is in no way straightforward. Being a woman in an all-boy profession, she seemed never to stop encountering workplace harassment exposure that did not only vivify her previous traumas but, most of all, had a devastating effect on her emotional well-being.

Her journey starts when she decides to move to Dubai for new opportunities in banking. After suffering rejection after rejection, Esa finally gets an offer to work at one of the world's top banks. But the high of this career break was soon worn out by the harsh reality of what she faced at work. Her first boss was an Indian man who always made sexist remarks about her appearance to her face, in front of other colleagues, during meetings. One day, while seated around a table with other male colleagues and male colleagues, she crossed a line she could not ignore by making a degrading comment that reduced her to nothing but her gender. She was shocked and humiliated, tried to get up straightened, but could not drive away the ache of his words.

It was not a one-time event. Day in and day out, her manager found ways to belittle her under the mask of professionalism. He would ask her to come to the office on Saturdays, a non-working day for most of the team. The loneliness, veiled intimidation, and sustained belittlement emotionally beat her down. She felt like a prisoner; if she were to complain, she would lose the very job that kept her from living.

It was only when her supervisor finally pushed her too far by making a sexual comment during an event for the team that Esa realized she had to take a stand. She filed a complaint at HR, but the outcome left her completely disillusioned with the place. The HR manager was another Indian and dismissed her complaint under the guise that her attire that day must have provoked him to say that about her. Esa couldn't speak further. How did her clothes deserve such harassment?

The emotional stress of the relentless harassment became unbearable. She wondered almost literally whether she was worthless; nothing could be done against such an entrenched system, as if it is amusing to treat this female differently than her male counterparts, who get strategic assignments, attend important meetings, and are respected while she's relegated to the side, with questioning condescending tones of "Can you handle this?" She'd wonder if it was a mistake to be a woman in a man's world.

The irony of it all is that despite this frustration from Esa, she was not an exception. She was later to witness the same treatment accorded to another female colleague, a young Pakistani woman, Rukhsar. She was relentlessly pursued by their line manager, a married man; he sent her inappropriate messages and flirted with her while saying that they were developing her as part of mentoring. Rukhsar told Esa about the harassment, her boss constantly asking her whereabouts, offering rides, and even sending her friend requests on social media. All of them were the same toxic cycle just with a different woman.

Just as Esa had demonstrated the courage of going public regarding the harassment, Rukhsar's complaint failed to bring about change and the atmosphere continued toxic, pushing Rukhsar out of the doors. Esa was once more brought to a grim reminder that in this world of 'great men', women working in their chosen field were forced to tolerate this without resistance. The system seemed to be rigged to shield offenders rather than victims.

Through all these experiences, she learned how to apply several survival techniques just to fit in with the trade. Initially, she would put in long hours on weekends and keep her head down, following all the ground rules because she thought that if she worked hard enough, she could be respected as much as her male colleagues. The more she struggled to perfect it, the more she was proved right-only this time with a sharp reminder: what it really was all about was her gender.

One of the toughest things she encountered was that she was in a world of men. It was the high-pressure sales world, and many of the men she networked with saw her more as an easy mark to manipulate rather than an equal who sought to enhance her career. She received countless propositions—men offering to help her get a job in exchange for drinks or dinner. The insinuation always hung in the air: If you want to succeed, you have to play the game.

She didn't like that her fellow male colleagues never had to face any such pressure. In fact, they were being able to give their undivided attention towards work, but she was required to furl off the advances coming her way as well as maintain her professional dignity. However, amidst this onslaught of harassment, Esa still found a glimmer of resilience. She learned how to recognize when men were trying to use her and learned to shut down these advances firmly, even though it meant closing potential doors into career opportunities. She was not willing to sacrifice her integrity for a job.

At times, it felt like an impossible battle lay ahead, how can one continue moving forward when the ground beneath one's feet is hostile? But with the spirit of beating exploitation, Esa learned to drive herself forward. She learned to assert herself without sinking too far in an industry that often treated her as not belonging.

Perhaps one of the most pivotal moments in Esa's emotional growth was when she received an unexpected message from Patrick, a man whom she once loved so very much. He was long gone from her life, and she had buried all that pain so many years ago as she continued moving ahead with her life. But this time, an unfamiliar Facebook notification made her notice: At first, she was ignoring this message, assuming it could have been one of those spam messages from any of her other friends reaching out to increase her friend total or maybe some really weird spammer. But a few days had passed when in her boredom and idle time, she opened the message.

She lowered her head, listening to the words. It was Patrick. She had changed her last name, and blocked him on all forms after they were done. She couldn't understand why he was reaching out to her after all these years, especially knowing he was a married man now. The thought of him calling her stirred a mix of confusion and frustration. He had chosen to marry the girl his mother had picked for him, moving on with his life while leaving her to heal from the heartbreak. So why now? Why was he trying to reconnect? The unanswered questions gnawed at her, and the more she thought about it, the more irritated she became. It felt like an invasion of the emotional distance she had worked so hard to create.

Yet, despite her irritation, a small part of her couldn't help but feel something else. It was a sense of wonder that he had still managed to find her. After all these years, after everything they had been through, he had somehow reached out. It was as if a thread from the past was still connecting them. The connection she thought had long since frayed. The thought that lingered stirred something deep within her. It was a mix of nostalgia and unresolved feelings she wasn't ready to confront.

He had found her Facebook account. After battling with the inner conflict, she finally brought herself to open the message. The message was very short but heart-wrenching message requesting a final meeting before he died. He wrote that he was ill and now wheelchair-bound. He didn't want to go to "that place" without seeing her one last time.

Esa wasn't moved by the message at first; her old wounds flared up as she reminisced about the heartbreak he had wrought. Patrick had broken her heart years ago, and she had worked religiously to mend it without him. The thought of reopening all those old wounds was like a heavy axe on her chest. She ignored the message for a long time, keeping it on the other side of her head as a belief: that she had healed; the past was far gone from her life.

But over time, the heaviness of his words finally dawned on him. He was coming not to see but to bid farewell. Patrick's health was failing, and he probably faced his last days. Esa spent her nights lying awake, torn between the anguish of her past and the compassion stirring in her heart. Could she face him again? Could she ever put aside the anger and hurt to let him have some peace in his last moments?

The internal battle continued, but with that and the overwhelming sadness that was inflicted upon him, he realized that even after the years and the pain that had been rained upon him, Patrick would have once meant the world to her. Now, she stood before the ultimate test of emotional growth whether to let go of the past or offer closure, not just for him, but for herself as well.

When Esa finally got wind of the fact that Patrick was dead, the pain crashed on her like a storm. She had been living her life beating into herself the fact that she had let go of that chapter of her life. Then came the word that he was gone never to return-forced upon her emotions she had buried long ago. All these emotions-the weights of unexpressed feelings, the regret for not being able to see him one last time, and finally death-washed her face at once. She hadn't realized how much she had wanted some form of closure from him, and now that door had closed.

The thought of Patrick dying without them ever getting to say goodbye to him torturing her. The guilt grew heavier with each passing day till she just couldn't bear to carry it any longer. She wanted to bid farewell not only to Patrick but to all the memories and emotions that had haunted her for years. In a moment of vulnerability, Esa decided to visit his grave. But she couldn't do it alone. She needed support, someone who knew her through all the ups and downs of her relationship with Patrick. That person was her mom.

She trembled as she approached her mother, too ashamed, too torn. "Mom," she said in a whisper, sorrowful voice, "I want to go to Patrick's grave. I didn't meet him before he died, and now I think I need to find some closure. I don't know.".

Her mother examined her, and read her gravity. "Why didn't you go see him?" she asked gently, already knowing the response but wanting to give Esa the chance to speak for herself.

"I resisted," Esa admitted, her voice shaking. "I told him it wasn't right for us to meet. He was a married man, and I had moved on with my life. I could not let myself be dragged back into the past. But now. now I feel like I was too harsh."

Her mother nodded, placing a reassuring hand on Esa's shoulder. "You did what you thought was the right thing to do at the time. It's okay to be upset. Okay, conflict is a better word," she said gently.

"I know," Esa whispered. "But I need to say goodbye. Will you come with me?

Her mother agreed without batting an eyelid; she could sense that this was something Esa needed to do, not only for Patrick but herself. Comforted by the quiet strength of her mother, Esa was more than happy to have her by her side now, more than ever.

Esa decided before heading out for the cemetery to dial Patrick's mother. She wanted to let her know and show sympathy regarding everything that had transpired. The communication was tense at first. Years ago, she has been quite harsh and judgmental of Esa, calling the breakup all her fault as well as speaking ill of her. But when she picked up the phone, Esa immediately sensed something was different about her.

"Esa, thanks for calling," Patrick's mother said, her voice trembling. "I want to apologise for everything. For how I treated you back then. I was wrong. I spoke badly of you and your mother. I blamed you for things that never had anything to do with you. And now, my son is gone. He's gone, and I know it was due to my bad conduct."

Esa was taken aback by the apology, yet she heard the genuine tears in the woman's voice. "It's okay," Esa spoke softly, straining not to cry too. "I know you were hurting back then.".

"No," his mother said, her voice breaking. "It's not right. I folded my hands and begged for forgiveness on your behalf too, regarding your mother. I accused you of making my son unhappy, and in the end, it was me who forced him into death. If only I were less strict, less merciless, then things would have been different."

This left Esa speechless. There was nothing that could be done to change the past, but at this moment, she felt her inner self begin to settle into peace. The bitterness that had brewed for years and somehow clouded their relationship was dissolving slowly.

When Esa stood before Patrick's grave in the cemetery, she did it silently with her mother. Though it hurt to stand there, seeing the pain curbed by her mother's stillness and the closure Esa had already felt about what was going on, Esa stood there knowing this moment-bloody thought it was necessary for healing.

She bid farewell to him as she was bidding farewell to the pain of the past.

The weight of her family burden-her mother was very ill, thanks to this situation, had fallen on her. In a moment, Esa faced a cocktail of pressures-her mother's health crisis and a toxic work environment. The vases that were about to break were Esa.

Life does not always stay on the right path, and sometimes, personal and professional responsibilities collide at the worst possible moment. Such a moment was when her mother had to undergo open-heart surgery, an emotionally charged experience for Esa and her family. The situation demanded juggling obligations—both to family and work—while navigating the profound stress of the mother's hospitalization and recovery. It was a period of learning as they sacrificed more, acquired responsibility, and tolerated the differences in work culture across countries.

The event started when Esa's sister called him from overseas and told his sister about the deteriorating condition of their mother and her need to undergo heart surgery.

The news about her mother was like receiving a devastating blow. She had undergone open-heart surgery, and the time was at its worst. She was already occupied with proving herself at work, and combating harassment at work, and was now paralyzed by fear about losing the most important person in her life. Then she was abroad, and it was unimaginable to ask her employer for leave from her job while travelling to India, particularly because of her tight agenda at work and flights being expensive. They thought maybe if they sent money, things would ease a little bit, and her family seemed to accept that. But she knew in her heart that her mother wanted her here physically. All the money in the world couldn't substitute for the emotional support she could extend by being there when the time of her mother's surgery came.

The fear gripped her—what if something went wrong? What if she couldn't be there for her mother at the time when she needed her most?

Amid all the mayhem, Esa did what she always did. She had to force herself to take that hard-earned decision, to travel to India. It was not an easy decision; she was working hard as there was a big report to be submitted. But she flew to India. She packed her laptop and intended to catch up on her work commitments while tending to her mother in the hospital. She knew that even in the hospital, she could not afford to be out of work. So she took her laptop to the hospital. The mission at stake was of paramount importance, and expectations were very high; family came first, however.

The next few days passed in the pressure cooker of tension and responsibility. Her mother's surgery took place at the National Heart Institute, where they accompanied her to every step through it, but even in the hospital work pressure was constant. She can remember sitting there in the recovery room working on her project. She recalls that her mom was unconscious just a few hours after her surgery. When she sat next to her bedside, she furiously typed reports into the night. Her laptop screen's glow was creating shadows on her tear-streaked face. Carrying mugs of coffee, she worked late into the night to meet their deadlines. Even though she was suffering from a personal crisis, professional demands would not subside and she had to go about doing her job. She was managing too much for any individual, and still, she felt that she could do nothing else. There was her mother who required her, and there was also her job demanding her attention. And it was at that moment when she realized just how hopelessly crushed she was.

The boss, being unmoved by her plight, piled on the pressure, asking her to attend meetings remotely while expecting similar levels of production with this personal crisis in tow. Esa's heart was torn between her duties as a daughter and the professional demands that showed no mercy for this once-stable child. The weight of it all feels suffocating yet somehow carried on.

She was torn between two things.

Firstly, there was an urge to be there completely for her mother during recovery. On the other hand, she simply could not afford to neglect her work and the subsequent missed deadlines. This balancing act made her realize that the current job was unsustainable for personal well-being and prompted her to start searching for a new position that would allow for a more manageable balance between personal crises and professional obligations. Along with these personal challenges, this time also witnessed the cultural differences in work environments.

As one who has worked in Indian and Arab corporate environments, the contrast stood out clearly in this very stressful situation. Managers in the Arab workplace are certainly harsh or blunt, but they are never cold-blooded. They appear to be more sympathetic to a person's personal problems than their Indian peers. In some corporate cultures abroad, the relationship can feel transactional at times, in which professional expectations completely overwhelm personal hardship. This realization helped her to understand what kind of culture she would like to associate herself with - one in which mutual respect and understanding existed between employees and management. She learned that though monetary support is crucial, at other times even physical presence at home cannot be replaced for loved ones. Equally important, she learned she should not sacrifice one side of the personal and work balancing act. Lessons from such a period of her life have since shaped her new perspective on work, family, and being in a better world with a supportive and empathetic culture at work.

All that would not have come without a heavy price; Esa had walked an eternal tightrope between burnout and emotional collapse, with all resistance exhausted in fighting the will of others during that time.

The surgery on her mother was a success, but no weight lifted off those shoulders; for work built into it the responsibility of carrying the family on one's back. In other words, her mother had expected much from her own family financially, alongside the personal and professional struggles she was to carry with her in Dubai.

There was a constant inner war: between giving in to the sense of total defeat from the situation and finding the strength to continue. Yes, one day she wished she quit. With all the harassment, discrimination, and emotional burdens of having to take care of the family, Esa felt she could no longer take all of this. Yet, even in such moments, inside, there was that flame of strength that would not allow her to quit.

As such struggles continued, Esa found a new strength. She feels that each harassment incident, setback, and disappointment made her determination to strive more. The industry might be hostile, but it would not break her. She has learned to fight back stand up for herself and others and keep going no matter how painful the journey was.

Esa's life story is a story of resilience-learning to find power in adversity, not letting workplace harassment and family responsibilities define her but instead shape her into one who is not defined by challenges but with strength that has made her emerge stronger, more determined, and clearer on worth. In short, her journey is far from over, but she has learned to know that she has within her the strength to overcome and win what comes her way.

Chapter 9: Grief, Closure, and Spiritual Awakening

Esa's life had been dotted with ups and downs, challenges and triumphs, but nothing would prepare her for the destructively tragic loss that would shape her future in ways that she couldn't yet understand. It all begins with a tragedy that changes everything and acts as a culmination of bereavement, resilience, and discovery.

Esa grew up in a relatively straightforward family where love and emotional upheaval crossed each other much more than that. There was a complicated relationship between her mother and her, one that was at times full of distance and limited expressions of love yet full of understanding. Her mother had married a Hindu man, which had generated tremendous tension-particularly in the context of a conservative society. Yet despite all these hassles, Esa always had a great deal of regard for her mother, considering her someone who led a really tough life but remained unbreakable.

Her sister got married and settled in Dubai. They have built a life there, and she even turned out to be a teacher. They had a lovely daughter, the little niece whom Esa adored. Their lives, once to say the least a little too chaotic, stabilized. Esa's brother also landed and stabilized himself. Yet in all this, her mother remained back in India.

Though very far away, Esa felt a heavy responsibility toward her mother. When Esa's mother's health began deteriorating, mainly from a diabetes diagnosis, Esa knew she would have to act. It was one of the toughest moments for Esa when her mother had to undergo heart surgery. It was a moment that brought about a significant shift in their relationship. Esa had flown all the way to India to be by her mother's side; here, she paid for her mother's surgery and stayed by her side.

"I remember that I had gone immediately. I paid for her surgery. I never thought twice about it. She cried and said, 'Among all my kids, I have never given you that love, that attention, but you've done beyond everything for me. I could never imagine you'd do this much for me.'

Those words took Esa by surprise. Her mother had never said so much as a word about there being an emotional distance between them, and Esa had never felt herself genuinely seen by her mother as until this day. But she told her now, in a tenderness she had rarely shown, "What are you talking about? You're my mother. You've always been my mother, and you're also my father now. Forget about this." From then on, their relation became deeper. They found common ground with the moments, unspoken conversations for so many years, and a mutual respect that had grown out of the troubles they both faced.

Life was getting better. Her sister was in Dubai, her brother had settled down, and Esa felt stability that she never known before. The surgery on her mother had been a success, and everything seemed to be back on track. It would just be the eve of her birthday, a night on June 20, and life would take a different turn.

Esa's sister had planned a surprise birthday party for her. The house was full of friends, loud laughter, and excitement. Esa was just getting ready, curling her hair in place and dressing up in a beautiful dress. Her sister had something planned; she did not know what, but the air was filled with something light she hadn't felt for years. It was, after all, to be a night of celebration, marking the beginning of something new for her.

She laced up her shoes and saw that her brother called at least three times. Her phone showed three missed calls from her mother's number. She was confused as to what was wrong with her brother.

She picked up the phone thinking it was a birthday wish, but on picking it up, the voice on the other end was heavy with grief.

"Mom died," said her brother.

Esa's world stopped. "What?" She whispered while she did not understand what exactly he had just said.

"Mom died," her brother repeated, his voice cracking.

For a moment, Esa was petrified in her body. Her friends were chatting around her; she felt an immediate change from their aspect because they noticed the change in her attitude. They asked what happened, but she still couldn't speak. She was in shock, unable to understand those words that had just been pronounced. The only word that could come out of her mouth, almost inaudible, was, "My mom died."

The party and the celebration around her all faded into the background. The only thing that felt important was how her mother was gone. That seemed impossible. Just a couple of days before things were fine. She had no way of knowing. Her mother just could not be gone this soon. She isn't ready for this. She wasn't ready to lose her.

Dazed, Esa grabbed her passport. She didn't cry-not yet. She thought only of going to India, of getting there fast. She had to see her mother. She had to be there. Her sister, her brother-in-law, and her niece were all included on the flight back. They all were going to be mourning, but Esa just couldn't feel anything, not yet.

When they finally arrived in India, she saw her mother's body in the icebox. She just looked like she was sleeping. There were no signs of death; no one thought that it was going to be their last. Esa could not believe it. She knelt beside her mother, looking at the calming expression on her face and willing her to wake up. But of course, she didn't.

As Esa prepared for her mother's funeral, she remembered a conversation they had had just before her mother died. "On my funeral," she had said, "I want to be buried in the Christian cemetery in Paharganj. All our family members are there." Her mother had been a woman of faith and it mattered a great deal to her that she was put to rest in that place where generations of her ancestors lay.

Esa wanted her mother's wishes to become reality. The funeral ceremony became a blur of tears and tears with a grief that was finally about to break out. She had spent years ignoring her mother, with all the time she had put into achieving her career in Dubai as the biggest factor; she hadn't been around for her mother when she really needed her. Now it was too late.

In the following weeks, Esa spiralled. The grief was too much to bear. She stopped eating. She stopped working. And she spent most of her days crying. "I felt like an orphan," she said. "I couldn't focus on anything. I wasn't myself anymore."

Her work in Dubai was not helping matters anymore either. Though sympathetic, her boss was pushing her to return to work. "'We know it's the greatest loss of your life,' he said, 'but we need you back.' Esa couldn't cope with all that. She was still in pain, still trying to make sense of her mother's sudden death. Going back to work wasn't possible. So she resigned. "Couldn't take it anymore," she said. "Didn't want that job."

For months Esa wandered in pain. She just could not move on, could not find a way to cope with the palpable sadness that had spread over her life like a shroud. She started practicing self-love exercises, that is, tuning inwardly to heal from the inside out. But that was not enough; the weight of her loss was too heavy, and she was drowning in it.

That night, Esa was at her breaking point. She was angry at God, at the universe, at everything that had taken her mother away from her. She prayed for answers, for some sign that her mother was okay, that she was at peace. "I was so mad at God," Esa said. "I just wanted to know where she was. I needed to know."

She spent that night crying to sleep. It must have been around 3:10 a.m. when the whispery voice against her ear woke her up. It was her mother's voice, the gentle, soothing voice that only she had ever known to be so full of comfort and love. "I'm okay," she said."I'm watching over you. You're not alone. You never will be."

The message was clear, and for the first time since her mother's death, Esa felt peaceful. Her mother wasn't gone. She still remained there, guiding her, watching over her, just as she had done in life. That was the turning point for Esa: life had to go on, even if grief came to knock at the door.

Esa was distraught; however, she had lost the entire family, and very slowly, her faith would seem like a vital element in the healing process. The mother always wished that she would turn towards God, take solace in the bible and embrace a spiritual way.

Although religion had kept Esa at arm's length for most of her adult life, after her mother's death, she found herself moving inexorably closer to it. It was as if the death of her mother propelled her as hard as it could toward the spirituality she'd always kept at a distance.

From that day on, Esa began rebuilding her life. She was sure to spiritual practices such as reading the Bible, praying, and maintaining her emotional and mental well-being. She quit drinking outright in order to observe her mother's wish.

It was reading the Bible not only as something dedicated to it but in the words of which she found her solace. Religion wasn't merely about religion, but rather about finding peace in all this serenity a feeling big and better than herself. The rituals, the prayers, and the quiet moments of worship became the anchors for her during these times she felt lost in almost everything she once knew.

Throughout her life, she had to oft face the bitter taste of rejections, especially in terms of faith and religion. Even while going through her own beliefs and Bible reading, she never helped but think the world would be a beautiful place if there were no dividing lines. Why was it that despite the fact that the color of blood is the same for all of humanity, people were so quick to judge and reject one another based on religious affiliations? Something that kept pounding in her head afterwards was people like Patrick's mother who dismissed people because they belonged to a different faith.

To Esa, faith had been an extremely personal concern, one of character, morals, values, and principles. Far from that which divides people, faith should be a great unifying factor. And yet, she witnessed how belief systems and practices drove separation and segregate people further from appreciating genuine and viable human contact and experience. These experiences left her disheartened and rejected for something fundamental, intrinsic in herself: her faith.

Through the painful encounters, Esa finally came to a deep realization concerning rejection and regret. Rejection, she realized, could be an incubator of fear, insecurity, and self-doubt. Evidently, rejection made her question her worth and place in the world. Yet, on the other hand, she began realizing if a person could work out those emotions, rejection could have a tremendous potential to transform into being a great force. It might also push forward personal growth, inspire resolve, and even strengthen who a person is. Esa chose rejection as a springboard to dedicate herself to honest living, true to her values and principles.

Regret, in contrast, was merciless and relentless; it lingers, gnawing away at the heart long after the moment has passed. Esa knew well that regret was much tougher to overcome because it emanated from not acting or standing up for oneself at the right time. That is why she was determined to do things the proper way, act rightly and genuinely, and even in secret to consider it a virtue to do it so. For her, rejection is something she can pass over, but she can't live with regret. And so, she stood up every time for the challenge with courage and on choice of authenticity over conformity and for self-respect over the dread of rejection.

Esa didn't just read the Bible; she sought to live its teachings, embodying its values and principles in her everyday life. She began attending church every Sunday, something she hadn't done in years. She was amazed at how welcome she felt, given everyone there had their story of loss and recovery. The church became a place of connection where her grief was meant, and her spiritual journey supported.

Esa's faith increased, but it was not a faith based on blind devotion or dogma; instead, it was finding strength in surrender. She learned there was power in letting go, trusting the universe had a plan, and just because things were coming apart at the seams, it wasn't everything falling apart. "Surrendering control was one of the hardest lessons I had to learn," she mused. "But once I did, things started changing.".

The loss of her mother had fired something inside Esa. A feeling she couldn't put a finger on at the time, but the months showed her that her sorrow had opened her heart even more than before. She was much more empathetic; she would see and feel so much suffering around her and tried to do her best about it.

And just the small ways: Esa started doing tiny acts of kindness. She began sharing her food with security guards, tipped delivery drivers more lavishly, and always offered a kind word to anyone crossing her path. These small moments were her way of giving back, of spreading the love she had received from her mother and others.

One day, after a friend threw up her hands and said, "You really should be doing something bigger," she had asked. Why don't you start volunteering? And Esa, never having considered it previously, must have let it bat around in her head for some time because before she knew it, it was coming to fruition.

She dived deep into work for social causes: water donations to those in need, visiting the orphanage, and participation in community outreach programs of her church. She was no longer healing herself; she was healing others along with herself. Every act of kindness was a step toward service, every moment of service a step toward healing.

As she became more involved in these activities, Esa felt a transformation within her; the grieving was still there but it no longer consumed her; rather, it became something else for her: it became purpose. "I realized that my mother's death didn't have to be only loss," Esa said. "It could be something new. It could be the beginning of something so that I could give back, and make her proud."

As Esa deepened her understanding of herself and her family history, she became aware of something that long had been hidden in plain sight: the generational patterns of suffering, fear, and insecurity which had shaped not only her life but the lives of generations before. It was a legacy of pain, inherited without ever knowing it.

Esa's mother had lived her life of strife. To the outside world, it would be misattributed as emotional distance but was actually a display of resilience. His father too, had lived his life of strife and had passed the weight of his own to his children, without ever intending to do so. For Esa, it was always just the way that life was: something to be endured, rather than something to be overcome.

Everything was different in the eyes of Esa once she lost her mother. She realized that this might be their generational curses—the cycles of trauma and suffering meant to break them and hopefully become freer. And if so, she was determined to be the first one in line to break them.

"I didn't want to live in fear anymore," said Esa. "I didn't want to operate out of a place of insecurity, of always feeling like I wasn't enough." She knew breaking these patterns would require deep work the kind of emotional and spiritual effort most people shy away from. But Esa was ready. Her mother's death had shown her that life was too short to stay in the shadows of the past.

Esa took it upon herself and started looking for more avenues to heal — therapies, meditations, and spiritual practices that could transcend the limits of the traditional religion. She got deeply into the concept of generational healing, where she realized that she had wounds in her life by and from her ancestors, and in healing herself, she thus heals those before her.

This was not easy to do. In some instances, Esa even felt the weightiness of the task at hand. But every time she was down, she remembered her mother's whisper during the night that she was not alone. And with that reminder, she found the strength to carry herself forward.

Chapter 10: Rebuilding Life: New Beginnings and Future Aspirations

For Esa, losing her mother meant that the whole world had changed overnight. It served to change her life in ways that were painful and transformative—casting a dark line through her grief but also propelling her into a journey of re-discovery. "The pain was so immense," she wrote in an essay that had captured a tender exhibit of recognition she called "When my world became my mother", "but within all this pain, she found a way to live again, to strive, to honour what her mom had taught her in life".

The road ahead was not an easy one, but Esa was out of the darkness of her suffering as well as into a new purpose. She wanted to live for her mother's values to live with intention and purpose. She realized that she was not just healing herself; she was healing others, too. This became her compass as she continued pushing forward in both her personal and professional life.

From being lost, she stood on firm ground. She has come out from the darkest period in her life stronger, more compassionate, and more self-actualized than ever before. Her mother's death was a catalyst for this change, and it was Esa's resilience that pushed her forward.

In Esa's first marathon, she was accompanied by a friend like a sister, one with whom she had been a confidante, appearing in her life when she needed her the most. Her name was Maram, a tall, stately woman at six feet, but their bond was strong and as strong as the bond between Jai and Veeru of yore, as in the iconic Indian film. Though she had been a distant friend for a number of years, she had never been at such a distance in Esa's heart. The universe must have created them because Maram entered Esa's life at the right moment for her to get out of this transformative phase.

Maram herself was a seasoned runner and had never won a marathon cup. And yet, when Esa crossed that finish line and held up that gold cup in her first marathon, Maram's joy knew no bounds. She hugged Esa with tears streaming down her eyes and said, "It feels like I have won too." It was a moment that crossed the boundaries of personal triumph; it was about mutual triumphs, about two friends raising each other up. For Esa, Maram was one of those people who somehow and kind of crop the kind of help the universe sends in order to mend our wounds—that is the kind of individuals who walk alongside us, cheering and celebrating every step we make.

Maram had signed Esa up for the marathon, giving her something to believe in when no one else would. She was Esa's biggest cheerleader, with support, love, and an occasional push when Esa really needed it. The marathon was not only a competition of their bodies but also Esa's journey to recovery and strength, and Maram has been a vital component of that process; they laughed, pulled each other up, and tried to make each other laugh.

Maram was more than a running partner to Esa; she was a sister, a soul, who also made her realize that even the healing path is never walked alone. The universe gifted that bond to her, reminding her that in the darkest times of our lives, we are never left without light.

Running marathons was something she would never have dreamed up as something she should do. "Out of nowhere," she said, "somebody told me to run a marathon. I'd never run in my life, but I did it."

It was not just a run in the marathon. She finished and won it, both happened at the same time. It was evidence of the strength and resilience within her, the same kind of strength her mother had always, to one degree or another, demonstrated.

The physical act of running was comparable to this inner act; both needed endurance, resilience, and an unwavering belief in oneself.

But even as she began slowly healing, something still seemed incomplete—her career.

Months later, Esa was thrilled to have gotten a job that was not perfect but was at least a start. She no longer needed to have everything under control; she trusted that things were bound to fall into place the way they were supposed to be. "You just surrender to the universe," she declared, reflecting on the lessons she learned. "You stop trying to control everything, and somehow it all starts to make sense."

Then, in the final stage, Esa began to thrive. She had risen through the ranks to great things, being promoted to head of department, which she felt a huge sense of pride in doing. She had travelled far from the person she was when her mom passed. But just as she thought she had overcome the worst, life had more in store for her.

It was different this time. Lessons from her past had made her stronger. She did not just bear things; she gradually grew stronger with each failure. Life's adversities became teachers who shaped her into a person who stood above adversity with power and grace.

It was in the hardest periods of her life that Esa found safety and strength in the solid friendship, which then became the rock for her. Maram, Dora, and 'J'made beacons guiding Esa through life, each bringing her own energy and love into Esa's life. Because of her infectious spirit and unwavering belief in Esa, 'J'took her off on trips to help her escape the shadows of her past. For example, she did everything for all of Esa's whimsical desires and even celebrated the minute success of hers; reminding her that life, after all, was meant to be lived to the fullest. That was how the turn in their Vietnam trip emerged; 'J'showed Esa the world through her eyes full of wonder, beauty, and possibilities. It was a journey of healing and self-discovery that helped piece Esa back together.

But Hermi was a friend who fought her own battles in a miserable marriage. Yet, to me, there seemed to be strength and independence in the possession of her own pain - a figure of strength. Witnessing how Hermi worked through her battles gave Esa perspective and strength. She learned that no matter how deep pain may be, it can also be tolerated and survived. To her, those are the friends that really stood like lifelines. Others were there for her in their own ways; they gave her little reminders every now and then that she was not alone on this whole thing. Their presence is a testament to the healing power of friendship and the profundity it infuses into one's life to have a community that lifts him up during the darkest of times.

It was Dora who would step up as some kind of guardian angel when Esa needed most, filling the vacuum caused by her mother's absence. Dora became more than a friend; she is a guardian angel whom Esa needed to visit her regularly while bringing along homemade meals and how Esa began to feel with her mother. Dora did not even give up on Esa when the latter tried her best to isolate herself from the world, getting disconnected with it altogether. Dora would then come knocking on her door, gently taking care, and making sure she'd eaten, and reassuring her gently whenever Esa felt submerged by her thoughts and emotions.

Dora made her feel that she belonged to the family again, especially with her family checking on her; she did not have to dread Dora saying things to them. It was through such little things that Esa emerged with the courage not to allow her past experiences and wounds to make her bitter. Dora's empathy and devotion led her to a place of healing wherein healing wasn't merely survival; it was an openness of trust to love and support once again.

Esa was at the dinner table when those were the words Dora would pen into his heart: "Esa, I have noticed that you sometimes flee from difficult conversations.". Never flee from them-face them and finally toss the emotional burden. For in that moment, as she finally found her voice through Dora, it was as if the universe finally spoke directly to her, telling her it was time to confront the pain she had been carrying with her for ages. It was a coming-of-age moment, a catalyst for change. Esa reflected on how she needed to confront what hurt her inwardly to be healed, not allow herself to be a captive of her past.

Dora was a way to demonstrate the love, patience, and care that her mom once bestowed upon her. It was such a friendship, such unreserved support, that reminded her she had enough worth and love when even hit at low points in life. And it was Dora's preservative presence that helped her believe in the possibility of healing, step by step, softly.

She was determined not to let her mother's death be the defining tragedy of her life, to instead live a life filled with purpose and meaning, in every sense of the word: a life that reflected the values that, despite never perhaps having been explicitly told to her, her mother had instilled in her.

In the end, Esa's story is as much a story of love as it is a story of loss. The ambivalent complicated love of the mother with her daughter was the bedrock of Esa's strength. It was even the source of healing for her, though she had not once realized it. She knew truths that her mother's death now revealed, truths she hadn't had time to discern because she was too busy being a grown-up, so to speak.

Now, she realized. Now that it was too late her mother had always been there guiding watching over her no matter at what distance their relationship stood. Even in her death, her presence was stronger than ever.

Esa wanted to not only heal but to grow, using her experiences as the fuel that would propel her forward. It was during this healing time that Esa made another life-altering decision: she would write a book about her journey.

Esa has always wished to be a writer. It was only when this proved to be her third-most traumatic experience that she actually decided to go ahead and do this book. Her mom once told her, "You live once. If there's something you want to do, don't think twice. Follow your gut and do it".

That word struck the core of Esa. She realized that the greatest way to glorify her mother's work, and by extension, her life, was to share this story with the world. She wanted other people to know, no matter how many times life knocks them down, that they can always rise again stronger and much tougher.

For Esa, book writing wasn't about telling her story but giving a piece of her soul to the rest of the world. It was both thrilling and terrifying to write about all these things and share them with people. It could be a challenge at times, but she felt there was something cathartic about it—something by which she would make sense of all she had undergone and inspire others to triumph over theirs.

This is the hardest thing Esa has ever written in the book. She dug into memories and dredge up emotions she had buried long ago. The pain, the loss, and the trauma all surfaced with it. There were moments when it seemed too raw, too overwhelming to put into words.

It was, however, through writing that she gained a certain amount of power over the self. It allowed her to set the framework for how she wanted it, to look at what she had learned and how she was strengthened by it all. She found the space to take back her story, not merely ripped back but learned from a position that was healing.

Some days the words were so fluid as if waiting there to be written. Other days the paper seemed a wall she could not climb. Yet amidst the ups and downs, Esa wrote on, knowing her story could help others. She knew through telling her own journey that she could bring hope to others who were fighting to be set free, just as she was.

Esa's motivation for writing this book was never for the purpose of reliving her experiences; she wanted to inspire others to transcend their own adversity and chase after dreams that seemed impossible. She declared that in the case of her life, while pain is inevitable, it does not have to define a man, and she had control over the choice of how she could respond to what challenged her at any given point in life.

In fact, Esa wanted to say to people through this book, "You are stronger than you know. You can overcome anything, no matter how insurmountable it seems." Effectively she wanted her readers to know that they were not alone in their struggle for the power would eventually rise above the darkness and find its way back into light.

It was also a way to celebrate Esa's mother. She taught her resilience, love, and never to give in, keeping up with the spirit she had always instilled in Esa about taking risks, following one's instinct, and living life on her own terms. This book was Esa's way of keeping her mother's spirit alive while sharing the wisdom she learned along the way.

The writing was therapeutic but difficult to accomplish. There are days when the writing flows easily, and then there are days that feel like one is climbing a very steep hill. And with all this writing, she was still learning how much of her story needed telling- not just to heal herself but to heal others.

It was for the person who was going to read her someday, the people who like her felt lost, broken or defeated. She envisioned sitting, reading comfort in her own words when they discover they aren't alone in the same pain. The vision kept her going, even on the hardest days.

But now, writing was no longer for the readers alone; it was about responsibility, and foremost, her mother's story. Esa wanted to do justice to her mother's memory, telling the world how much her mother had moulded her and how deep their relationship was.

Although she was still writing her book, Esa did feel a kind of closure on certain chapters of her life. In itself, the act of writing had been healing; it helped her digest and make peace with those events that had shaped her.

She knew that the book was accomplished, and she could attest to her strength, resilience, and growth. Yet, most of all, she was hoping it would empower others to be inspired and find hope if they needed to hear her story.

For Esa, writing this book was a journey in itself. She knew that life had many more challenges in store for her, but she also knew that she was strong enough to face them. With every word she wrote, healed, and grew into, she felt more empowered to move forward than ever before.

This was not just a book about looking back, but it was also a book about creating a future filled with hope love and purpose for Esa.

Chapter 11: Conclusion

The story of Esa is much more than a history of suffering and loss but rather a living testimony of the human capacity to survive, to be resilient, and indeed transform. I remember her tough background to the experiences that moulded her being, and it is with Esa's life that an example of rising from the dregs of despair into a new strength and purpose can be truly exemplified.

By sharing Esa's story, I am reminded of the universal truths we often forget as adversity descends upon us. Life is what we know, unpredictable, and full of challenges and setbacks that get out of our control sometimes. Yet it is during these moments, perhaps when we feel most vulnerable and broken, that provides an opportunity for growth and renewal. Esa's story makes this a truth to be told with beatific eloquence, showing us that even in our greatest moment of suffering, we have the power of choice over how we choose to respond.

Life has been one thing after another to Esa-from the overwhelmingly crushing loss of her mother to trying trials that no mortal on earth could stop her from finding. Every chapter of life has thrown a test of strength and challenged the darkest corners of her soul. However, each time she emerges more sturdily, more painfully self-aware, and more determined to have a life that would serve as an antidote to pain, as it is with love, purpose, and fulfilment.

The most significant lesson I learned from Esa's life would be self-belief. She has witnessed moments too numerous to count where her doubt, fear, and insecurity could have easily consumed her. She did the opposite; she chose to find faith in herself and possessed the courage to strive for her aspirations in the presence of obstacles.

This reminds me deeply, and I hope it reminds you too: it is these moments of being most repeatedly told we are not enough that we need most to recall that our worth will not be found in what happens to us or what others think of us. Esa reminds us that we all have strength inside that can catapult us out of tough situations if only we dare to tap into them.

According to Esa, courage is not the absence of fear but being able to move on despite it. It was either leaving her job, facing her grief head-on, or doing something to write a book and share her story with the entire world, and Esa constantly chose to act bravely. She never let her fears paralyze her; she used them all to propel her toward her goals.

Another important lesson learned from Esa's experience is to risks. Her mother's phrase remained with her for all of her life: "You live once. If there's something you want to do, don't think twice. Follow your gut and do it.". Whether it was the risk of changing careers, the danger of running a marathon she never could, or the risk of opening her heart to the rest of the world through her writing, Esa has continually embraced risk as an essential part of growth.

However, in life, sticking to the familiar may bring safety, but it does not bring greater rewards. It is beyond one's comfort zone and where one would take the risk of trying and often intuition guides that the greatest rewards are obtained. More than that, through risks, we grow, find our true direction, and create meaningful fulfilment for our lives.

It's this, if anything, that Esa would want her readers to learn from her journey: take risks. Whether it's a new career, a step away from poisonous relationships, or just a long-held dream, bold steps can change your life in ways you could never have imagined.

At the heart of Esa's tale is love. It is love that has sustained her through some of the darkest moments in her life and love that continues to propel her forward into the future. But ultimately, it is the love of her mother that gives her strength and inspiration. And even in death, her mother lingers, reminding Esa that she never really alone is.

Perhaps the greatest thing Esa's story teaches us is that love is the most powerful thing we possess. It heals wounds, offers to mend broken spirits, and even hopes when all seems desolate. It was love-that of her mother, at any rate-which finally let Esa rise from the hollow of her grief. But it is also the love she now bears for herself and for the world about her which holds her up to date.

Esa learnt that love was not something we receive from other people, but something we can make in ourselves. In such small gestures of giving towards people who were like strangers to us, the community she has forged and the mercy in which she nurses people in pain, Esa follows in her mother's footsteps. She lives life shaped by the principles, the patterns, of love and selflessness.

But as you reflect on Esa's story, I hope you'll be reminded of the power of love in your own life. Whether it is the love of a family member, a friend, or even the love you show to yourself, that force has the potential to transform your world. Love is the foundation of resilience; it is the fuel that keeps us going forward, even in those times when life feels unbearable.

In the end, Esa's journey is one with hope in that, after all the failures, disappointments, and detours, she still moves forward full of optimism and purpose. Her life can be an example for many in the reality that however dark the road ahead may be, something always shines at the end.

This is the legacy Esa wishes to be left behind not for her only, but for her readers as well. She wants a story about being strong, taking a leap of faith, and pursuing life with much strength, then living with intensity, courage, and conviction. Above all, she wants people to know that amid loss and hardship, there is hope. There is always the possibility for renewal, healing, and growth.

As Esa moves into her new future, she does so knowing that she is never alone. Her mother's voice continues to echo in her heart, reminding her that she has the strength inside her to overcome all that life laid in her path. And it is with this knowledge that she moves out; with confidence and resilience full of hope for what is ahead.

This is the greatest gift that her mother could bequeath her: the knowledge that love is unending, that resilience is possible, and that, in the end, we are never really alone. It's a lesson Esa carries with her each day, and it's a lesson she hopes to share with the rest of the world through her story.

Verses Kindler Publication

Reach us through our website -
https://www.verseskindlerpublication.com/
For more information visit our Instagram or Facebook page.